THE ENGLISH HANDBOOK

OF

GRAMMAR, STYLE,

AND

COMPOSITION

Staff of Research and Education Association,

Dr. M. Fogiel, Director

 Research and Education Association
505 Eighth Avenue
New York, N. Y. 10018

THE ENGLISH HANDBOOK OF GRAMMAR,
STYLE, AND COMPOSITION

Printed in the United States of America

Library of Congress Catalog Card Number 83-62275

International Standard Book Number 0-87891-552-4

PREFACE

The ability to write and speak correctly and effectively is a prerequisite for doing well in all subjects in school including math, the physical sciences, and the social sciences. Writing and speaking skills become very important also when seeking a job and trying to succeed in a chosen career.

Despite the publication of hundreds of books in the English field, each one intended to provide an improvement over previous books, students have found English grammar and writing a difficult subject to understand and learn. This results from the numerous different rules governing proper grammar and writing in addition to the confusion which results from the many exceptions to these rules.

English books currently available will usually explain a standard rule or definition in a few pages written by a professional grammarian who has a technical insight of the subject not shared by students. The explanation is often written in an abstract manner which leaves the student confused as to the application of the rule. The examples usually following the explanation of a specific topic are too few in number to enable the student to obtain a thorough grasp of the concept involved.

The present *Handbook* does not use the hard-to-understand technical jargon usually found in English grammar books. Rather, it is written in an easy-to-understand, straight-forward manner. Hundreds of practical examples have been included to enable the student to see what is correct and what is wrong in all areas of English. Exercises are included at the end of every chapter for review.

The first section of this *Handbook* is devoted to the "building blocks" of good English — the "Parts of Speech". These include separate chapters on nouns, pronouns, verbs, adjectives and adverbs, prepositions and conjunctions. The next section is entirely devoted to the "Sentence" and the "Paragraph". The section begins with parts of the sentence, structural problems, and errors in style. The second part of this section covers figures of speech, mood and voice. The last part of this section deals with the "Paragraph" which includes choosing a topic sentence, unity of the paragraph, and finally, conveying the tone of the paragraph.

The third section of the *Handbook* concentrates on the "mechanics" of good English — "Punctuation". This section is divided into three parts: the stop, the pause, and clarification. The stop includes the period, exclamation point, and question mark. The pause covers the comma, semicolon, colon, dash, and parantheses. Clarification deals with quotation marks, apostrophe, italics, capitalization, hyphens, brackets, and numbers.

The fourth section of the *Handbook* covers "Spelling" which includes word analysis, spelling lists, spelling rules, prefixes, and suffixes. The section concludes with proofreading.

The *Handbook* devotes an entire chapter on "How To Write A Paper". The chapter covers the form of the paper, purpose and point of the paper, writing an outline, selecting an introduction, writing the body of the paper, and finally, writing the conclusion. A special section on getting the most out of the Dictionary as a reference source has also been included in the first chapter of this *Handbook*.

To meet the objectives of the book, the specialties of many staff members of REA were drawn on for contributions. Gratitude is expressed to them for their efforts, as well as to the numerous contributors who devoted brief periods of time to this work.

The difficult task of coordinating the efforts of all persons was carried out by Carl Fuchs. He also contributed much to the organization of the subject matter, review, and design of the book.

Max Fogiel, Ph.D.
Program Director

CONTENTS

CHAPTER 1

INTRODUCTION

1.1 ENGLISH GRAMMAR

English grammar is a set of rules or conventions that helps to guide correct written and spoken English.

Good grammar is like good table manners. It varies with circumstances, but something about it always remains constant.

When speaking, the language used varies naturally, depending on the person spoken to. But although the word choice changes when speaking to parents, friends or policemen, the goal is still the same: communication of ideas. In this book, standard English and usage is fully explained. This language is expected in formal writing and speech. But as a writer and a speaker, judgment is also necessary. Sometimes colloquial English is more appropriate than standard.

If the same set of grammatical rules is understood by each individual, written and spoken expression becomes much easier. Knowledge of the English language is not just the understanding of words and their meanings. Grammar is a technical vocabulary, which gives added meanings and functions to words. In fact, each word in the English language can be classified as a part of speech depending on the role it plays in a sentence. A word is either a noun, pronoun, verb, adjective, adverb, preposition, conjunction, or interjection.

Grammar, then, is a set of conventions about writing and speaking. It is a product of the way people spoke in the

1

past and of the way people are speaking now. Although it changes, and many rules of grammar are obscure, for the most part there is a consensus about correct and incorrect English. This book can help put the reader in touch with what is standard and correct English usage.

1.2 WRITING A PAPER

1.2.1 THE FORM OF THE PAPER

When preparing a manuscript use standard size paper, $8\frac{1}{2}$ x 11 inches. Use unruled paper for typewritten papers and ruled paper for handwritten ones. Always use white paper. Colored paper is unacceptable.

If the paper is handwritten, write legibly and avoid ornate handwriting. Often, skipping a space between lines makes the job of reading and correcting much easier. Blue or black ink is standard when writing.

If the paper is typed, type neatly by avoiding extensive crossouts and erasures. Also make sure that the ribbon is fresh and that the type is clear. When typing, double space between lines. Use one inch margins on all sides of the paper. Indent five spaces at the beginning of each paragraph. Leave one space between words and two spaces after end punctuation. Never begin a line with a punctuation mark that belongs at the end of the preceding line.

Number pages consecutively with arabic numerals in the upper right-hand corner, except for the first page number ("1") which appears centered at the bottom of the page.

If deletions or corrections are necessary, draw a horizontal line through the material. If typing, a capital "M" may be used over the deletion. If a correction or additional material is needed, mark the insertion with a caret ($\wedge$) and write the insertion above the caret.

Center the title on the first line of the first page approximately two inches from the top of the page. Leave about one inch between the title and the first line of the paper. Thereafter, do not repeat the title on the other pages. Do not underline the title or enclose it in quotation marks unless the title is a quotation itself. A period is not used after a title although a question mark or exclamation point can be used when desired.

When writing or typing, the division of a word at the end of a line often becomes necessary. For easy reading, it is best to avoid awkward division of a word. The following are some rules for syllabication and hyphenation.

1. Never divide a one syllable word such as *height*, *sixth*, *cleaned*, *fixed*. When the _-ed_ ending is added to form the past tense, do not split it off when it is not pronounced as a syllable.

2. Never divide a word so that a single letter stands by itself: *speed-/y*, *read-/y*, *a-/gent*, *i-/ambic*.

3. Avoid dividing proper names.

4. Avoid separating a name and the initials that go with it.

If a division of a word is necessary, divide the word between syllables and place the hyphen at the end of the line. Syllabication can be checked in the dictionary. (see "USING THE DICTIONARY.")

1. Divide compound words on the hyphen. Avoid adding a second hyphen. For example, not *ex-pres-/ident*, but *ex-/president*, not *self-in-/flicted*, but *self-/inflicted*.

2. Words with prefixes should be divided on the prefix: *non-/aligned*, *pre-/war*.

3. Words with suffixes should be divided at the suffix: *grate-/ful*, *joy-/less*.

Remember that the form of the paper often makes the first impression on the reader. A writer's dedication is often indicated by the way the work is presented. Also, when a writer has followed standard rules of form, the reader need not be concerned with or distracted by these basic mechanics and can therefore concentrate on the material itself.

1.3 PLANNING THE PAPER

1.3.1 PURPOSE AND POINT

The writing process actually begins at the very moment a paper is assigned. As the writer's mind begins to think of a subject, ideas and thoughts are already being formed. That is why the preparation for writing a paper is so important. Often, these first ideas will stay with the writer--they need to be well thought out to see if they are workable.

Many things should influence the choice of a subject by the writer. When a teacher assigns a paper, certain restrictions are often placed on the student. If the length of the paper is established, this should have a direct bearing on the subject. For example, can the subject "Causes of World War II" be adequately treated in a three page essay? A writer must learn to limit his subject. Also, does the subject lend itself to the assignment? Would such a theme as the influence of the Beatles on the sixties generation be an appropriate topic for a research paper? These questions must be answered by the student before any writing is done. But perhaps the most important question in the choice of a subject is interest. If a writer knows little about a topic he (or she) must ask one basic question: "Do I have enough curiosity to investigate this topic further?" Nothing is more tedious than writing about something which is of no interest. This boredom is often expressed in the style of the writing and the reader will also suffer.

Once a subject has been chosen, the purpose of the paper must be defined. Usually papers are written to <u>explain</u>, <u>persuade</u>, <u>tell a story</u>, or <u>describe</u> some object, experience, or theory.

If surfing is the subject of a paper, for example, the writer might <u>explain</u> what surfing is or how it is done. Likewise, one could try to <u>persuade</u> the reader to surf or not to surf. A <u>story</u> could be told of some famous or exceptional surfer, or else of an outstanding incident in one's own surfing experience. A <u>description</u> of the subjective experience of surfing is another possibility.

After defining the purpose of the paper, the point of the paper must be established. What end is the writer trying to achieve? Although the point might be obvious, it is still a good idea to summarize it in <u>one sentence</u>.

If the subject is fishing, for example, and the purpose is to explain what fishing is and how it is done, a point must now be established. Certainly, it is not just to write a collection of facts about fishing. This would be boring even to a fisherman. The writer should return to his interest in the topic. If the writer has knowledge about the subject, for example, there must also be some general feelings on the subject. A conclusion is drawn or an observation made which links all the facts in the paper together. If the writer enjoys fishing, this could become the point of the paper.

Some examples of subjects, purposes, and points are given below.

Subject: Sewing

Purpose: To describe how it felt to sew my sister's wedding dress.

Point: Being able to sew made it possible for me to have an exciting experience.

Subject: Submarines

Purpose: To explain how submarines work.

Point: Submarines work on very simple principles.

Subject: Summer camp

Purpose: To tell the story of an awful experience at summer camp.

Point: Summer camp is not always fun.

A writer should be in no rush to get to the typewriter. Inspiration alone is rarely the source of a good paper. If writing is the craft of expressing ideas, then the writer must have clear ideas to begin with. Take time to think and organize before going into a frenzy of writing.

1.3.2 WRITING AN OUTLINE

Making an outline is the next logical step in preparing a paper. It requires only a short time to prepare and helps tremendously when actually writing the paper. Writing a paper without an outline is like taking a walk through a strange city without a map. The destination might be reached, but only by chance. With a map, the traveller can know his way in advance. Similarly, an outline is a plan; it guides the writer through the paper with clear and logical steps.

When writing an outline, the writer should note all thoughts on the subject in short phrases, considering whether they contribute to the purpose and point of the paper. Returning to the surfing example, a writer might want to explain what surfing is and why it is enjoyable. The following thoughts might occur:

> surfing is fun
>
> you need a board
>
> what the board is made of
>
> length and weight of the board
>
> how to learn
>
> where surfing came from
>
> you can surf on Long Island, but it is better in Hawaii

The next step is organization. First, group the ideas. Many entries concern the board. Group them under the main heading "The Board." Then four other points remain: surfing is fun, learning to surf, history of surfing, and good places to surf. Along with " The Board," these become the main points. They are the main points because they cannot be grouped under any other heading. These are the major headings; all other points will fall under one of these.

These main points must be organized. The order must be logical to both the writer and the reader. They should develop, or work towards, an end.

The following is a sample outline for the surfing paper.

> Introduction
>
> Surfing is fun
>
> The board
>
>> why you need it
>>
>> its length and weight
>>
>> what it is made of
>
> How to learn to surf

History of surfing

Best places to surf

Now, in looking over the outline, the writer might decide to spend the major part of the paper discussing the board and how to learn, and make the last two sections rather short. Or, one might decide to make all the sections about the same length, except the first one, which should be relatively short since it is a general introduction to the paper. Decisions of this nature should be made before any writing is done.

1.3.3 INTRODUCTION OF THE PAPER

The introduction should bring the reader into the paper. It should indicate the general idea of the paper (the 'thesis'), and make it sound as interesting as possible. Here are some examples:

> *Anyone who was a child can remember hearing fairy tales. Each nation on earth has fairy tales. But strange as those stories may be, they are not as strange as the fact that fairy tales are the same the world over. They are always the same stories in different words and the same characters in different clothes.*

> *Shakespeare's most thought-provoking play is* Hamlet. *It has given rise to more varied and contradictory interpretations than any of his other plays. One point that few can agree on is Hamlet's insanity: Was it feigned or real?*

1.3.4 WRITING THE PAPER

When writing the paper, the author should be guided by the outline. The actual process of writing should be a time of expanding and articulating those ideas sketched out in the outline. The writer should make sure that the paper is focused and that transitions between paragraphs are clear. This copy, however, should only be the first draft of the paper. It is essential to read the paper over. Most of the simple errors of agreement, misspelling, and sentence fragments can be caught by the writer. This is also the time for any major revision that the paper might require. After all the necessary corrections have been made, the revised version should be neatly copied or typed. Finally, the paper should be reread once again for any additional corrections.

1.3.5 CONCLUSION OF THE PAPER

If a paper is well thought out and focused, the conclusion should be fairly easy to write. It sums up the paper, touches on the main points, and makes a final statement about the subject. It works in such a way that the reader not only feels he knows what he has read, but understands the point of the paper. Not only is a conclusion a summary, it is the last part in a chain of thought or reasoning. Some sample conclusions appear below.

In spite of the bugs, the cold, the rain, and my wife's endless nagging, the trip really was a lot of fun.

We have seen that Mr. Jones' interpretation of Hamlet has very little to do with the play itself. Mr. Jones tells much about Sigmund Freud and his theories, but very little about Shakespeare's Hamlet.

Once again we see how a trivial incident can have large and unexpected consequences.

1.4 USING THE DICTIONARY

1.4.1 USING THE RIGHT WORD

Writing is a form of communication, and simply enough, the most effective writing is clear and concise. That is why a writer must continually strive for precise expression and economy of language by finding the exact word to express a specific meaning. Here, the dictionary becomes indispensable.

1.4.2 SIMILAR FORMS AND SOUNDS

The complex nature of language sometimes makes writing difficult. Words often become confusing when they have similar forms and sounds. Indeed the author may have a correct meaning in mind, but an incorrect word choice can alter the meaning of the sentence or even make it totally illogical.

> NO: *Martha was always part of that <u>cliché</u>.*
>
> YES: *Martha was always part of that <u>clique</u>.*
>
> (A <u>cliché</u> is a trite or hackneyed expression; a <u>clique</u> is an exclusive group of people.)
>
> NO: *The minister spoke of the soul's <u>immorality</u>.*
>
> YES: *The minister spoke of the soul's <u>immortality</u>.*
>
> (<u>Immorality</u> means wickedness; <u>immortality</u> means imperishable or unending life.)
>
> NO: *Where is the nearest <u>stationary</u> store?*
>
> YES: *Where is the nearest <u>stationery</u> store?*
>
> (<u>Stationary</u> means immovable; <u>Stationery</u> is paper used for writing.)

Below are groups of words that are often confused because of their similar forms and sounds.

1. accent-- v. to stress or emphasize. (*You must <u>accent</u> the last syllable.*)

   ascent-- n. a climb or rise. (*John's <u>ascent</u> of the mountain was dangerous.*)

   assent-- n. consent, compliance. (*We need your <u>assent</u> before we can go ahead with the plans.*)

2. accept-- v. to take something offered. (*She <u>accepted</u> the gift.*)

   except-- prep. other than, but. (*Everyone was included in the plans <u>except</u> him.*)

3. advice-- n. opinion given as to what to do or how to handle a situation.
   (*Her sister gave her <u>advice</u> on what to say at the interview.*)

   advise-- v. to counsel. (*John's guidance counselor <u>advised</u>*

him on which colleges to apply to.)

4. affect--   v. to influence.   *(Mary's suggestion did not affect me.)*

    effect--   v. to cause to happen.   *(The plan was effected with great success.)*
                n. result.   *(The effect of the medicine is excellent.)*

5. allusion--   n. indirect reference.   *(In the poem, there are many Biblical allusions.)*

    illusion--   n. false idea or conception; belief or opinion not in accord with the facts.
                (Greg was under the illusion that he could win the race after missing three weeks of practice.)

6. already--   adv. previously.   *(I had already read that novel.)*

    all ready--   adv. + adj. prepared.   *(The family was all ready to leave on vacation.)*

7. altar--   n. table or stand used in religious rites.
                (The priest stood at the altar.)

    alter--   v. to change.   *(Their plans were altered during the strike.)*

8. capital--   n. 1. a city where the government meets.   *(The senators had a meeting in Albany, the capital of New York.)*
                2. money used in business.   *(They had enough capital to develop the industry.)*

    capitol--   n. building in which the legislature meets.   *(Senator Brown gave a speech at the Capitol in Washington.)*

9. choose--   v. to select.   *(Which camera did you choose?)*

    chose--   *(past tense, choose.)*   *(Susan chose to stay home.)*

10. cite--   v. to quote.   *(The student cited evidence from the text.)*

    site--   n. location   *(They chose the site where the house would be built.)*

11. clothes--   n. garments.   *(Because she got caught in the rain, her clothes were wet.)*

    cloths--   n. pieces of material.   *(The cloths were used to wash the windows.)*

12.	coarse--	adj. rough, unrefined. (*Sandpaper is coarse.*)
	course--	n.1. path of action. (*She did not know what course would solve the problem.*) 2. passage. (*We took the long course to the lake.*) 3. series of studies. (*We both enrolled in the physics course.*) 4. part of a meal. (*She served a five course meal.*)
13.	consul--	n. a person appointed by the government to live in a foreign city and represent the citizenry and business interests of his native country there. (*The consul was appointed to Naples, Italy.*)
	council--	n. a group used for discussion, advisement. (*The council decided to accept his letter of resignation.*)
	counsel--	v. to advise. (*He offered counsel to Jerry.*)
14.	decent--	adj. proper; respectable. (*He was very decent about the entire matter.*)
	descent--	n.1. moving down. (*In Dante's Inferno, the descent into Hell was depicted graphically.*) 2. ancestry. (*He is of Irish descent.*)
15.	device--	n.1. plan; scheme. (*The device helped her win the race.*) 2. invention. (*We bought a device that opens the garage door automatically.*)
	devise--	v. to contrive. (*He devised a plan so John could not win.*)
16.	emigrate--	v. to go away from a country. (*Many Japanese emigrated from Japan in the late 1800s.*)
	immigrate--	v. to come into a country. (*Her relatives immigrated to the United States after World War I.*)
17.	eminent--	n. prominent. (*He is an eminent member of the community.*)
	imminent--	adj. impending. (*The decision is imminent.*)
	immanent--	adj. existing within. (*Maggie believed that religious spirit is immanent in human beings.*)
18.	fair--	adj. 1. beautiful. (*She was a fair maiden.*) 2. just. (*She tried to be fair.*) n.3. festival. (*There were many games at the fair.*)

fare--	n. amount of money paid for transportation. (*The city proposed that the subway fare be raised.*)	

19. forth--   adv. onward. (*The soldiers moved forth in the blinding snow.*)

      fourth--   n. adj. 4th (*She was the fourth runner-up in the beauty contest.*)

20. its--   possessive form of *it*. (*Our town must improve its roads.*)

      it's--   contraction of *it is*. (*It's time to leave the party.*)

21. later--   adj., adv. at a subsequent date. (*We will take a vacation later this year.*)

      latter--   n. second of the two. (*Susan can visit Monday or Tuesday. The latter however, is preferable.*)

22. lead--   n. (*led*) 1. a metal. (*The handgun was made of lead.*) v.t. 2. (*leed*) to show the way. (*The camp counselor leads the way to the picnic grounds.*)

      led--   past tense of *lead* (*#2 above*) (*The dog led the way.*)

23. loose--   adj. free, unrestricted. (*The dog was let loose by accident.*)

      lose--   v. to suffer the loss of. (*He was afraid he would lose the race.*)

24. moral--   adj.1. virtuous. (*She is a moral woman with high ethical standards.*) n.2. lesson taught by a story, incident, etc. (*Most fables end with a moral.*)

      morale--   n. mental condition. (*After the team lost the game, their morale was low.*)

25. of--   (prep.) from (*She is of French descent.*)

      off--   adj. away, at a distance. (*The cowboy rode off into the sunset.*)

26. passed--   v. having satisfied some requirement. (*He passed the test.*)

      past--   (pp of *pass*) 1. over. (*Tom's problems were past.*) n.2. the history or former life of a person, group, institution, etc. (*The United States has a relatively short past compared to other nations.)*

27. personal-- adj. private. *(Jack was unwilling to discuss his childhood; it was too personal.)*

    personnel--n. staff. *(The personnel at the department store was made up of young adults.)*

28. principal-- n. head of a school. *(The principal addressed the graduating class.)*

    principle-- n. the ultimate source, origin, or cause of something; a law, truth. *(The principles of physics were reviewed in class today.)*

29. prophecy--n. prediction of the future. *(His prophecy that he would become a doctor came true.)*

    prophesy--v. to declare or predict. *(He prophesied that we would win the lottery.)*

30. quiet-- adj. still; calm. *(At night all is quiet.)*

    quite-- adv. really, truly. *(She is quite a good singer.)*

    quit-- v. to free oneself. *(Peter had little time to spare so he quit the chorus.)*

31. respectfully-- adv. with respect, honor, esteem. *(He declined the offer respectfully.)*

    respectively-- adv. in the order mentioned. *(Jack, Susan and Jim, who are members of the club, were elected president, vice-president, and secretary respectively.)*

32. stationary-- adj. immovable. *(The park bench is stationary.)*

    stationery-- n. paper used for writing. *(The invitations were printed on yellow stationery.)*

33. straight-- adj. not curved. *(The road was straight.)*

    strait-- adj. restricted, narrow, confined. *(The patient was put in a strait jacket.)* n.2. narrow waterway. *(He sailed through the Straits of Magellan.)*

34. than-- conjunction used most commonly in comparisons. *(Maggie is older than I.)*

    then-- adv. soon afterward. *(We lived in Boston, then we moved to New York.)*

35. their-- possessive form of *they.* *(That is their house on Tenafly Drive.)*

they're--	contraction of *they are.* <u>*(They're* leaving for California next week.)</u>
there--	adv. at that place. *(Who is standing <u>there</u> under the tree?)*
36.	to--	(prep.) in the direction of; toward; as *(She made a turn <u>to</u> the right on Norman Street.)*
	too--	adv.1. more than enough. *(She served <u>too</u> much for dinner.)* 2. also. *(He is going to Maine <u>too</u>.)*
	two--	n. 2; one and one. *(We have <u>two</u> pet rabbits.)*
37.	weather--	n. the general condition of the atmosphere. *(The <u>weather</u> is expected to be clear on Sunday.)*
	whether--	conj. if it be a case or fact. *(We don't know <u>whether</u> the trains are late.)*
38.	who's--	contraction; *who* and *is; who* and *has.* <u>*(Who's* willing to volunteer for the night shift?)*</u>
	whose--	possessive form of *who.* *(<u>Whose</u> book is this?)*
39.	your--	possessive form of *you.* *(Is this <u>your</u> seat?)*
	you're--	contraction of *you* and *are.* *(I know <u>you're</u> going to do well on the test.)*

1.4.3 CORRECT MEANING

Often a writer uses a word which <u>seems</u> correct in a particular context, but actually does not express the author's true meaning. As you will see in the following examples, there may be subtle differences in word definitions. That is why it is always helpful to use the dictionary.

NO: He had <u>illusions</u> of grandeur.

YES: He had <u>delusions</u> of grandeur.

(<u>Illusion</u> suggests the false perception or interpretation of something that has objective existence. For example: *The magician performed an optical <u>illusion</u>.* <u>Delusion</u> implies a belief in something that is contrary to fact or reality, resulting from deception or misconception.)

NO: Joseph listened <u>intensely</u> to what he said.

YES: *Joseph listened <u>intently</u> to what he said.*

(<u>Intensely</u> means earnestly, fervently, zealously. For example; *He was <u>intensely</u> involved in the cause.* Intently means firmly directed or fixed.)

NO: *I <u>imply</u> from your letter that you will not be attending the meeting next week.*

YES: *I <u>infer</u> from your letter that you will not be attening the meeting next week.*

(<u>Imply</u> means to suggest something. For example; *I <u>implied</u> that I didn't approve of their actions.* <u>Infer</u> means to draw a suggestion from a remark or action.)

1.4.4 DENOTATION AND CONNOTATION

Language can become even more complicated. Not only can a single word have numerous definitions and subtle meanings, it may also take on added meanings through implication. The <u>denotation</u> of a word is the direct explicit meaning. The <u>connotation</u> is the idea suggested by its place near or association with other words or phrases.

<u>Example</u>: Child-like and <u>childish</u> both have the denotation of "like or characteristic of a child." However, the two words have their own connotations.

<u>child-like</u>-suggests the favorable qualities considered typical of a child: innocence and trustworthiness, for example. <u>Child-like</u> is generally favorable on all age levels.

<u>childish</u>-- connotes the unfavorable characteristics of a child: foolishness or immaturity, for example. When applied to adults, <u>childish</u> is almost invariably a term of reproach.

Often a word's connotation will be fully explained in the dictionary. Yet the <u>context</u> of the word can also help to reveal the general and added meanings. The context is the part of the statement in which the word or passage at issue occurs; that which leads up to and follows a particular expression. Compare the following sentences.

EXAMPLES:

1. *The actress perfectly captured the character's <u>child-like</u> qualities in her performance.*

2. *Your <u>childish</u> behavior is quite annoying in a grown person.*

However, the literal and the implied meaning of a word can also blend and change with time. Take the word <u>bureaucracy</u>, for example.

Literal meaning: 1.a. Administration of a government chiefly through bureaus staffed with non-elected officials.
b. The officials staffing such bureaus.

Yet when speaking of <u>bureaucracy</u> in government <u>today</u>, many are more likely to comment on the red tape of bureaucracy and the inflexibility and inefficiency of the system rather than the structure of the system itself. Compare the following sentences. Which use of the word bureaucracy is more familiar to you?

EXAMPLES:

1. <u>Bureaucracy</u> is a common feature of many governments.

2. Knowing the <u>bureaucracy</u>, I won't receive my income tax refund for many months.

When reading and writing, try to understand and use words to their fullest by taking into account the connotation, denotation, context, and time period in which the word is used.

1.4.5 CLEAR WRITING

The dictionary is the place to find the exact word you want to use. In writing try to express yourself precisely. Avoid using vague words. Compare the following pairs of sentences for clarity.

NO: What is his <u>angle</u> on the Middle East crisis?

YES: What are his <u>ideas</u> on the Middle East crisis?

NO: *It is difficult for Ellen to* <u>deal</u> *with the pressures of college.*

YES: *It is difficult for Ellen to* <u>cope</u> *with the pressures of college.*

NO: *I do not* <u>get</u> *the solution.*

YES: *I do not* <u>understand</u> *the solution.*

NO: *This passage from the text* <u>shows</u> *the character's true nature.*

YES: *This passage from the text* <u>illustrates</u> *the character's true nature.*

The dictionary is a reliable source because it is exact. Words through everday use often take on meanings that are incorrect and imprecise.

1.4.6 WHAT THE DICTIONARY TELLS US

1. PROPER SPELLING

The dictionary is the place to look when one is not sure how to spell a word (see "SPELLING USING DICTIONARY.")

There are some words that have more than one correct spelling. These forms, which are equally acceptable, are separated in the dictionary by a comma or the word <u>or</u>. Some examples are: <u>*modeled*</u>, <u>*modelled*</u>; <u>*judgment*</u>, <u>*judgement*</u>; <u>*align*</u>, <u>*aline*</u>; <u>*catalog*</u>, <u>*catalogue*</u>. If a spelling is not as acceptable as another, the word <u>*also*</u> will precede the less acceptable spelling: *color, Also* <u>*colour*</u>. British spellings are often given after the American spelling and are also set off by a comma: <u>*theater*</u>, <u>*theatre*</u>; <u>*connection*</u>, <u>*connexion*</u>; <u>*favor*</u>, <u>*favour*</u>.

Other variant spellings (like <u>nite</u> for <u>night</u>, <u>thru</u> for <u>through</u>), are not listed in most dictionaries and are not acceptable spellings in formal writing.

2. SYLLABICATION

Each word listed in the dictionary is broken into syllables. Most dictionaries divide words by printing a centered period between the syllables. For example, *cat·e·gory, cat·er·pil·lar*. Other dictionaries use the centered period and an accent mark to divide the word where the syllable is accented: *par´i·ty, ren'e·gade*.

When the division of a word is necessary, it should be made between syllables. This helps the reader to make a smooth transition from one line to the next. For a complete list of rules for syllabication and hyphenation see "WRITING A PAPER."

> NO: *Andrea doesn't understand anyth-ing mechanical.*
>
> YES: *Andrea doesn't understand any-thing mechanical.*
>
> NO: *Could that speech insp-ire anyone?*
>
> YES: *Could that speech in-spire anyone?*
>
> NO: *There is room for another pa-ssenger on this train.*
>
> YES: *There is room for another pas-senger on this train.*

3. PRONUNCIATION

Following each word in bold face is the correct pronunciation in parentheses. The dictionary uses accent marks to indicate which syllables are accented; diacritical marks to create the sounds of the vowels; and phonetic spellings to help sound the words out. Even the pronunciations are syllabicated for clarity.

EXAMPLES:

> *easy (ē·zē)*
>
> *pass (pás)*

There is a guide at the beginning of the dictionary and/or at the bottom of each page explaining these symbols.

Also, if the word has more than one acceptable pronunciation, the most common form is listed first.

4. PARTS OF SPEECH

The eight traditional parts of speech are used to help identify the words in the dictionary. The following is a list of the abbreviations used.

> <u>n.</u> *(noun)*   <u>conj.</u> *(conjunction)*
>
> <u>adj.</u> *(adjective)*   <u>prep.</u> *(preposition)*

adv. (adverb)   v. (verb)

pron. (pronoun)   interj. (interjection)

Inflected forms are indicated by the following abbreviations:

sing. (singular)   pl. (plural)

obj. (objective)   poss. (possessive)

fem. (feminine)   masc. (masculine)

Inflected forms that are irregular or pose a spelling or pronunciation problem are given in brackets immediately after the part of speech.

EXAMPLES:

datum (dā´təm, dat´əm)n. [pl. DATA (-tə, -ə]
(Here the inflected form is given because the plural form is irregular.)

who (hoo), pron. [obj. WHOM (hoom), poss. WHOSE (hooz).]

(In this example the case form is irregular.)

good (good), adj. [BETTER (bet´er), BEST (best)]

(The comparative and superlative form of the adjective is formed irregularly in this example.)

The abbreviations tr. and intr. are used to indicate whether a verb is transitive or intransitive.

The dictionary will also list other special forms or uses of a specific word. For example, ease can be either a noun or a verb. Earthy has a comparative (earthier) and a superlative (earthiest) form. The various forms of a word are listed under the main word in a combined entry.

5. THE DEFINITION

A word frequently has more than one meaning. A good dictionary will list all possible definitions. Often examples of usage will be given to help clarify each meaning. Also used in the definition are synonyms, words with approximately the same definitions, and sometimes antonyms, words with opposite meanings.

19

for the word *insanity, lunacy* is given as a synonym

for the word *exile, banish* is given as a synonym

for the word *noisy, quiet* is given as an antonym

for the word *bad, moral* is given as an antonym

When checking a definition, always read through the various meanings to make sure you have made the correct word choice.

6. ETYMOLOGY

Since the English language is based on many other languages, most standard dictionaries give the origin or etymology of each word. A word's origin is indicated by an abbreviation, which can be checked at the beginning of the dictionary. Many etymologies are interesting, especially for a foreign language student who may recognize the original form of many English words.

EXAMPLES:

defective (Fr. défectif) is originally derived from the French language.

justice (M.E. justise) has its origin in Middle English.

bazaar (Per. bázǔr) is taken from the Persian language.

1.4.7 THE DICTIONARY AS A REFERENCE SOURCE

Most dictionaries have many separate sections which cover a wide range of topics. There are often entries on biographic and historic names, foreign words and phrases, rhyming dictionaries, mythological names, abbreviations, usage, grammar and other features. Keep in mind that the dictionary is a good, all-round reference source.

7. IDIOMATIC LANGUAGE

Idiomatic language is characteristic of a certain language, region, group of people, etc. The dictionary will give those idiomatic expressions which are most common to the English language. Since these expressions often cannot be translated word for word, it is wise to check their definitions if you are unsure of the meaning. Could you determine the meaning of "run of the mill" by literally translating its parts? Idiomatically it means "ordinary." The following are some other examples of idiomatic expressions.

EXAMPLES:

> *to run across*-- *to encounter by chance*
>
> *to run for it*--*to run in order to escape or avoid something*
>
> *to pull through*-- *to get over an illness or through*
>   *a difficult time*
>
> *to make up to*--*to flatter, or try to be agreeable to*

For additional information on idioms, see "Prepositions".

8. SPECIAL WORDS

To help identify words more completely, the dictionary uses geographical, subject, and usage labels. A geographical label such as Brit. (British) or Scot. (Scottish), indicates that the word is characteristic of a certain region or language. The subject label indicates that the word belongs to a specialized field of activity: Physics or Cooking, for example. Finally, there are numerous usage labels: Obsolete, Archaic, for instance.

A special label on a word usually indicates that it is not a part of average and everyday vocabulary. If a word is labeled Archaic, Obsolete, Slang, Rare, Dialect, Vulgar, etc., avoid using it in formal writing. Words that belong to a special vocabulary such as nautical terms or biological terms should be used in technical writing. Perhaps one of the most important aspects of writing is the reader. It is important to choose words that make sense to both the reader and yourself. The dictionary can help you do this.

1.4.8 THE THESAURUS

As an additional reference source, a thesaurus can be invaluable. To avoid repetition, or to formalize a piece of writing, for example, a writer often needs a slightly different word than the one in mind. A thesaurus is an ideal solution for such problems. It is a book composed entirely of classified synonyms and antonyms. Many thesauri are in dictionary form; the synonyms follow the main word as illustrated in the examples below. Often, a thesaurus will also refer the writer to other related words.

EXAMPLES:

> *beneficial*, adj. *valuable, helpful, salutary, useful, advantageous. See GOOD, USE.*

> *infirm*, adj. *feeble, decrepit; unsound, failing. See WEAKNESS.*

> *manager*, n. *superintendent, supervisor, overseer. See DIRECTOR.*

1.5 EXERCISES

A. Find the alternative spelling of the following words. Decide whether one spelling is more commonly used or acceptable.

1. meter
2. adviser
3. judgment
4. theatre
5. peddler

B. Determine the etymology of the following words.

1. mascara
2. delicatessen
3. macaroni
4. pattern
5. purple

C. Find two synonyms for the following words. Also identify the part of speech corresponding to each word.

1. knowledge
2. bulwark
3. earthly
4. latent
5. magic

D. What labels accompany the following words? Specifically, what kind of label is used in each case? (Subject, usage, geographical)

1. irregardless
2. o'er
3. adventive
4. disc
5. molt
6. beaver

1.5 EXERCISES

    7. jussive

    8. kine

    9. alienor

  10. kid

E. This exercise tests your ability to use the dictionary.

    1. Write the plural of isthmus.

    2. Where is Hälsingborg and what is its population?

    3. What is the meaning of the abbreviation EbN?

    4. What are the comparative and superlative forms of good?

    5. What is the capital of Iran?

    6. How many syllables does ornamentation have? Divide the word at its syllables.

    7. What does the French term "carte blanche" mean?

    8. Write the pronunciations of data using diacritical marks. Which pronunciation do you use?

    9. When was the Industrial Workers of the World founded?

  10. Write the plural of radius.

  11. Where does the accent fall on meager?

  12. What is the alternate spelling of gang?

  13. Write the plural of stratum.

  14. Who was Ralph Waldo Emerson?

  15. What is the feminine form of blond?

  16. What does in the long run mean?

  17. Write the pronunciations of finance. Which pronunciation do you use?

  18. Where does the accent fall on innocent?

  19. How many syllables does awaken have? Divide the word at its syllables.

  20. What is Avogadro's number?

CHAPTER 2

THE NOUN

A noun is a part of speech that names a person, place, thing, idea, animal, quality or action. Along with verbs, nouns are the principal elements of any sentence.

> Into each <u>life</u> some <u>rain</u> must fall.
>
> On his <u>vacation</u> in <u>California</u>, <u>Jason</u> called his <u>sister</u>.
>
> <u>John</u> gave the <u>men</u> their <u>money</u> for the <u>work</u>.

All the underlined words in the above sentences are examples of nouns. Just as people can be classified according to a number of characteristics such as hair color, height, weight, occupation, income or nationality, so can nouns be classified according to specific characteristics.

2.1 PROPER AND COMMON NOUNS

Most nouns are common nouns. They name any one of a class or kind of people, places or things. A proper noun is the official name of a particular person, place or thing. The writer's main problem with proper nouns is recognizing them so they can be capitalized. (See Capitalization)

Proper nouns include:

PERSONAL NAMES:

Mr. William Jones   *Susan Lee Gray*

Dr. Harrison   *Captain Smith*

John Mills, Jr.	*Mrs. Laurence*
Zeus	*St. Francis*
Pope Paul	*President Roosevelt*

NAMES OF NATIONALITIES AND RELIGIONS:

Frenchman	*Judaism*
Englishman	*Catholicism*
Mexican	*Christianity*

GEOGRAPHIC NAMES:

Paris	*Seine River*
New York City	*England*
Peking	*Mount Wilson*

NAMES OF HOLIDAYS:

Christmas	*Rosh Hashana*
Columbus Day	*Thanksgiving Day*

NAMES OF TIME UNITS:

Monday	*February*

The writer should be careful not to capitalize common nouns simply to add legitimacy or distinction. Compare:

PROPER

COMMON

PROPER	COMMON
Let's go Saturday.	*What day should we go?*
It was February.	*It was during the winter.*
The bears are in Canada.	*This country is beautiful.*
Ask the Australian.	*Ask that man.*
James is Catholic.	*What is your religion?*
I saw the Colorado River.	*That river I saw was clear.*
St. Francis taught here.	*She was made a saint when she died.*

2.2 CONCRETE AND ABSTRACT NOUNS

A noun that names a member of a class, a group of people, places or things is a <u>concrete noun</u>, because what it names is physical, visible and tangible. <u>Abstract nouns</u> name a quality or mental concept, something intangible that exists only in our minds. Compare:

CONCRETE NOUNS	ABSTRACT NOUNS
book	*truth*
rose	*beauty*
Susan	*mankind*
court	*justice*
sentence	*thought*
newspaper	*idea*
girl	*love*

2.3 COLLECTIVE NOUNS

A noun used to describe a group of people or things that is considered a single unit is called a <u>collective noun</u>. Some examples are:

orchestra	*family*	*band*
herd	*flock*	*chorus*
committee	*audience*	*gang*
Congress	*crowd*	*multitude*
faculty	*staff*	*personnel*
crew	*team*	*group*
government	*press*	*bunch*
class	*nation*	
majority	*jury*	

The difficulty with collective nouns is trying to decide whether to use the singular or plural verb form. When the emphasis is on the collection, the singular is used, as in:

> *The* <u>*orchestra*</u> *plays at noon every day.*

But if the emphasis is on the individual members of the group, the plural verb is required.

> *The* <u>*orchestra*</u> *are unable to work well together.*

Therefore, the meaning of the sentence will determine which form is correct. This problem will be treated in more detail in the discussion of agreement between the subject and the verb.

Collective nouns can be used in the plural form:

> *The* <u>*teams*</u> *are ready to begin.*
>
> *I heard both* <u>*orchestras*</u> *last night.*
>
> *The* <u>*governments*</u> *of both countries agree.*
>
> *How many* <u>*committees*</u> *voted for the amendment?*

2.4 COUNTABLE AND NONCOUNTABLE NOUNS

Most nouns can be made plural by changing the ending (usually by adding "s"). These are called <u>countable nouns</u>. There is a group of nouns, however, that has no plural. These are called <u>noncountable nouns</u> since the members of the group they represent are either singular or plural depending on the context. Two main groups of noncountable nouns are:

1. MASS NOUNS:

cheese	*moss*	*coffee*
dust	*wine*	*measles*
wheat	*grass*	*clothing*
furniture	*bedding*	*tea*
gold	*clover*	*corn*

milk   dirt   hay

These are nouns that describe concrete objects considered in a mass quantity.

2. ABSTRACT NOUNS:

courage	*truth*
fun	*news*
information	*advice*
economics	*biology*
mathematics	*jazz*

Occasionally, some of these nouns take a plural form if a variance of the object described is stressed:

How many <u>cheeses</u> (different kinds) did you taste?

That store carries more <u>teas</u> (kinds of) than any I've seen.

There can be many <u>truths</u> on a subject.

The <u>mosses</u> of Vermont and Florida are different.

2.5 THE FUNCTION OF NOUNS IN A SENTENCE

The function of the noun determines its position in a sentence. It can fulfill many different functions including:

1. Subject
2. Object (indirect or direct)
3. Complement (subjective or objective)
4. Object of preposition
5. Appositive
6. Modifier to another noun
7. Modifier of an adjective or verb

A detailed description of these functions and how they can be recognized in a sentence will be found under "THE PARTS OF THE SENTENCE."

2.6 NOUN COMPOUNDS

A compound is a group of words (usually two) that functions as a single part of speech.

> Her mother-in-law watched closely as the blackbirds fluttered about the birdbath behind the flower garden.
>
> That store clerk had no common sense; he took the traveler's check without even checking the signature on a credit card.

Noun compounds generally take one of the following forms:

NOUN AND NOUN:

birdbath	credit card
book store	author-editor
father figure	basketball
headache	notebook
doghouse	living room
seat belt	season ticket
reform school	policeman

ADJECTIVE AND NOUN:

blackbird	common sense
greenhouse	vice-president
anybody	half brother
everything	

POSSESSIVE NOUN AND NOUN:

traveler's check	cook's assistant
mother's helper	citizens' committee
child's play	

NOUN AND PREPOSITIONAL PHRASE:

mother-in-law
Queen of England
life-of-the-party
House of Representatives
breach of promise
philosophy of life
woman-of-the-world

editor-in-chief
stick-in-the-mud
fly-by-night
stream of consciousness
right of way
man-about-town

NOUN, CONJUNCTION AND NOUN:

trial and error
breaking and entering
bread and butter
stress and strain

VERB AND NOUN:

search warrant
punchball
pitch fork
driftwood

breakfast
dump truck
stoplight

GERUND AND NOUN:

firing squad
living room
swimming pool
spinning wheel
shopping center

managing editor
leading man
housing project
chewing gum
breaking point

NOUN AND VERB:

handclasp
ice skate
backpack

toothpick
ski jump
lifeguard

PREPOSITION AND NOUN:

downpour	*afterthought*
uproar	*underwear*
bypass	*undergraduate*
overview	

NOUN AND GERUND:

problem solving	*decision making*
housecleaning	*mind reading*
handwriting	*peacekeeping*
fly-fishing	*filmmaking*
dressmaking	*scuba diving*

VERB AND ADVERBIAL PREPOSITION:

break-in	*cleanup*
go-ahead	*chin-up*
fill-in	*breakout*
crackdown	*pickup*
lockup	*layoff*
showdown	*stopover*

There are a number of other less common compound forms. Some compound verbs can become noun compounds; adding an "er" to them indicates the "doer" of the action described:

fortune-teller	*pawnbroker*
baby-sitter	*lawgiver*
peacemaker	*troubleshooter*
ice skater	*pressure cooker*

Compound words cause problems because they are formed in so many different, often illogical, ways. They can be written as one word, two words, or a hyphenated word, although the hyphenated form is less common. As soon as a compound word becomes generally accepted as a term, it is written as one word. However, the only way to be sure of the accepted spelling of compound words is to consult a dictionary.

2.7 CHANGES IN FORM--Inflection

In some languages, nouns can change their form and thereby slightly change their meaning. Usually, the change in form is effected by adding special endings. The term used to describe the change of form of a word is <u>inflection</u>. Inflected forms include:

I. <u>Number</u>--endings that tell whether a noun is singular or plural, but occasionally the plural is formed by a change within the structure of the word itself.

II. <u>Case</u>--alterations within a word which show a change in the relationship between that word and the other words in the sentence. Different case forms are used depending on whether the word functions as a subject, object, modifier or some other part of speech. Some languages have as many as 20 cases. In English, however, there are only three:

		Pronoun	Noun
1.	the nominative	*I will go.*	*John will go.*
2.	the objective	*Go with me.*	*Go with John.*
3.	the possessive	*It is mine.*	*It is John's.*

Because the noun does not change form according to whether it is nominative or objective, these two cases will be discussed along with the pronoun cases, which do change form from the nominative to the objective case. The noun changes only in the possessive case, which is used to indicate possession.

To summarize, the English noun has only two inflective forms:

1. <u>Number</u>: changes to indicate plurals

2. <u>Possessive case</u>: endings to indicate possession

2.7.1 GENDER

In English there are four genders. They are not indicated by inflective forms but by entirely different words.

Masculine	Feminine	Common (either sex)	Neuter (no sex)
father	*mother*	*parent*	*marriage*

uncle	*aunt*	*cousin*	*friendship*
brother	*sister*	*dancer*	*tree*
John	*Martha*	*driver*	*desk*
rooster	*hen*	*animal*	*zoo*

2.7.2 NUMBER--PLURAL NOUNS

Most nouns can be singular or plural. The usual plural form adds "s" to the end of the word:

desk	*desks*	*book*	*books*
girl	*girls*	*lamp*	*lamps*
guest	*guests*	*idea*	*ideas*
letter	*letters*	*smile*	*smiles*

However, there are many exceptions to this guideline. After "y" preceded by a consonant, "y" changes to "i" and "es" is added:

forty	*forties*	*ecstasy*	*ecstasies*
lady	*ladies*	*category*	*categories*
country	*countries*	*sky*	*skies*
baby	*babies*	*secretary*	*secretaries*
cabby	*cabbies*	*berry*	*berries*
economy	*economies*	*fairy*	*fairies*

If the final "y" is preceded by a vowel, no change is made and the plural is formed by adding "s":

money	*moneys*	*decoy*	*decoys*
buy	*buys*	*guy*	*guys*
attorney	*attorneys*	*abbey*	*abbeys*
valley	*valleys*	*boy*	*boys*
volley	*volleys*	*monkey*	*monkeys*

If the last sound in the word is "s", "z" "ch" "sh" or "x", an "es" is added. The "es" is added so the word can be easily pronounced.

class	*classes*	*branch*	*branches*

box	*boxes*	*dish*	*dishes*
kiss	*kisses*	*fish*	*fishes*
fox	*foxes*	*ranch*	*ranches*
watch	*watches*	*match*	*matches*

However, if the "ch" is pronounced "k", only "s" is added:

stomach	*stomachs*
monarch	*monarchs*
epoch	*epochs*

Often the final "fe" or "f" in one syllable words becomes "ves":

half	*halves*
wife	*wives*
life	*lives*
leaf	*leaves*
hoof	*hooves*
calf	*calves*

There are exceptions, of course:

chief	*chiefs*
roof	*roofs*

Many nouns have plural forms that are irregular:

child	*children*	*goose*	*geese*
sheep	*sheep*	*cherub*	*cherubim*
mouse	*mice*	*deer*	*deer*
series	*series*	*man*	*men*
foot	*feet*	*ox*	*oxen*

For nouns ending in *o* add *-s* or *-es* to form the plural. These spellings must be memorized individually.

solo, solos	*tomato, tomatoes*
piano, pianos	*potato, potatoes*
studio, studios	

Finally, there are a number of foreign words that have become part of the language that retain their foreign plural form. There is a trend that Anglicizes the spelling of some of these plural forms by adding "s" to the singular noun. In the list that follows, the letter(s) in parentheses indicate the second acceptable spelling as listed by Webster's New Collegiate Dictionary.

axis	*axes*
radius	*radii (radiuses)*
bureau	*bureaux (s)*
plateau	*plateaux (s)*
larva	*larvae (s)*
vertebra	*vertebrae (s)*
crisis	*crises*
parenthesis	*parentheses*
criterion	*criteria (s)*
phenomenon	*phenomena (s)*
vortex	*vortices (es)*
matrix	*matrices (es)*
memorandum	*memorandums (a)*
stratum	*strata*
symposium	*symposia (s)*
millenium	*millenia (s)*
appendix	*appendices (es)*

As you can see, there are many peculiarities associated with plural formation. It is advisable to have a dictionary on hand to check plural forms.

2.7.3 THE POSSESSIVE CASE

1. The possessive case of nouns is formed by adding an apostrophe and an "s" to words that do not end with an "s" or a "z" sound:

a fox's cunning	*anyone's choice*
the girl's dress	*the tree's leaves*
somebody's letter	*the mother's hope*
the room's color	*the men's store*

the children's game	*the M.D.'s charges*
one's desire	*anybody else's way*
nobody's business	*our school's record*
Jeannie's grades	*Mr. Smith's hopes*

The preference is to add only an apostrophe to words when they end in an "s" or "z" sound:

a lioness' strength	*the lynx' tail*
the boys' bicycles	*the crocus' growth*
the girls' dresses	*the Roberts' address*
his mistress' eyes	*the hostess' gown*
for goodness' sake	*Dickens' story*
M.D.s' theories	*the Jones' house*

However, it is also acceptable to add "s" if the sound is not unpleasant or difficult to pronounce:

a lioness's strength	*the lynx's tail*
his mistress's eyes	*crocus's growth*
the Roberts's address	*the hostess's gown*
Dickens's story	*the Jones's house*

NOT	*the boys's bicycles*	*the girls's dresses*
	for goodness's sake	*the M.D.s's theories*

It is the sound that determines whether to add "'s" or only " ' ".

There is a final group of words that merits attention since they end in an "s" sound, but do not end in "s", "x" or "z", and so are easy to miss. However, if you pronounce these words aloud you will have no problem in making them possessive with only an apostrophe:

for conscience' sake	*at his patience' end*
for appearance' sake	

2. THE "OF" PHRASE

When the possessive form refers to an animate object, such as a person, the addition of ' or 's to the noun is the standard procedure. However, an "of" phrase is most often preferred when the possession refers to an inanimate object.

Therefore, we write:

the color of the cup	*NOT--the cup's color*
the lines of the paper	*NOT--the paper's lines*
the flavor of the sauce	*NOT--the sauce's flavor*
the intricacy of the pattern	*NOT--the pattern's intricacy*
the make of the car	*NOT--the car's make*
the painter of the picture	*NOT--the picture's painter*
the writer of the book	*NOT--the book's writer*

Inanimate things do not possess. Unfortunately, this guideline has its own exceptions. There are many occasions when we use the possessive form to indicate possession for nouns referring to things.

EXCEPTIONS

Expressions of time:

the year's end	*a day's work*
the week's pay	*today's weather*
three weeks' notice	*a month's time*
a moment's hesitation	*two days' journey*
an hour's wait	

Nature:

the tree's roots	*the moon's phases*
the earth's atmosphere	*the star's light*
the flower's beauty	*the river's roar*

Money or measure:

a dollar's worth	*an arm's length*
your money's worth	*a stone's throw*

Groups of people:

the newspaper's headlines	*the restaurant's employees*
the ship's crew	*the crowd's response*
the union's stand	*the city's parks*

the country's flag *the nation's concern*

There is no clear rule. Besides the idioms mentioned, there are numerous others that appear to violate even the most reliable rules:

the book's success *the policy's failure*

the razor's edge *the bank's cashier*

the car's brakes *the candle's glow*

The "of" phrase is sometimes used with nouns referring to animate objects, especially to modify a long or awkward construction and to avoid a piling up of possessives.

NO: *The dog's collar's latch was broken.*

YES: *The latch of the dog's collar was broken.*

NO: *The postman's mailcart's bag's handle slipped.*

YES: *The handle of the postman's mailcart bag slipped.*

NO: *The team's captain's signals to the players began slowly.*

YES: *The signals of the team's captain began slowly.*

NO: *The class's secretary's report to the teacher was long.*

YES: *The report of the class secretary was long.*

NO: *An old grey dog's very long and furry coat...*

YES: *The very long and furry coat of the old grey dog...*

Any name consisting of several words that would be awkward in the possessive also uses the "of" phrase:

NO: *The director of the Health, Education and Welfare Department's message to the President...*

YES: *The message of the director of the Health, Education and Welfare Department to the President...*

NO: *The small business committee of the Equal Employment Opportunity Commission's guidelines...*

YES: *The guidelines of the small business committee of the Equal Employment Opportunity Commission...*

NO: *The local chapter of the Girl Scouts of America's meeting will be on Friday.*

> YES: *The meeting of the local chapter of the Girl Scouts of America will be on Friday.*

Always try to keep the reader or the listener in mind; use the construction that will convey your meaning most clearly.

3. POSSESSIVES IN A SERIES:

When one of the words in a series is a possessive, all of the other words in that series must also be in the possessive case:

> NO: *Bill, Henry, George and my new restaurant...*
>
> YES: *Bill's, Henry's, George's and my new restaurant...*

> NO: *Andy, Dick and her report...*
>
> YES: *Andy's, Dick's and her report...*

> NO: *Ms. Smith and your car...*
>
> YES: *Ms. Smith's and your car...*

4. JOINT POSSESSION —DIFFERENT POSSESSION

Joint possession is also used when each word in a series possesses something different:

> NO: *James and Michael's paintings are similar.*
>
> YES: *James' and Michael's paintings are similar.*

> NO: *The chefs and chauffeurs' uniforms continue to last.*
>
> YES: *The chefs' and chauffeurs' uniforms continue to last.*

> NO: *The taxi drivers, bus drivers and traffic policemen's jobs are in demand.*
>
> YES: *The taxi drivers', bus drivers' and traffic policemen's jobs are in demand.*

> NO: *The secretary and the boss's explanations differed greatly.*
>
> YES: *The secretary's and the boss's explanation differed greatly.*

> NO: *Were the producer's and the directors complaints justified?*

YES: *Were the producer's and the director's complaints justified?*

JOINT POSSESSION—SIMILAR POSSESSION

When each word in a possessive series owns the same thing, the possessive is formed on the last word only:

> NO: *Let's go over to John's and Mary's house.*
> (If you made "house" plural, you would be visiting two houses.)
>
> YES: *Let's go over to John and Mary's house.*

> NO: *Susan's and Jill's vacation was an exciting one.*
> (If they went on separate vacations, "vacation" would have to be plural; "was" would become "were" and "one" "ones".)
>
> YES: *Susan and Jill's vacation was an exciting one.*
>
> NO: *He is Mr. Lang's and Mr. Harriman's tailor.*
>
> YES: *He is Mr. Lang and Mr. Harriman's tailor.*

5. POSSESSION WITH GERUNDS

A gerund looks like a verb, but is used as a noun. It is the "ing" form of the verb. The participle looks like a gerund, since it also ends in "ing", but it serves as an adjective, not as a noun. (See "verbals" for further explanation of these terms).

When a noun or a pronoun immediately precedes a gerund it is usually possessive:

> *His arriving when he did pleased us all.*
>
> *The Senators' voting was divided.*
>
> *New York's hitting was better than Boston's that day.*
>
> *The urgency of Mary's screaming surprised him.*
>
> *What do you think of your sister's writing?*

However, if the word preceding the gerund is an inanimate object, we use the "of" phrase since it is usually accepted that inanimate objects do not possess.

> NO: *The car's starting delighted Susan.*
>
> YES: *The starting of the car delighted Susan.*

NO: He thought nothing of the rug's shampooing.

YES: He thought nothing of the shampooing of the rug.

NO: When they saw the building's burning, they applauded.

YES: When they saw the burning of the building, they applauded.

6. PARALLEL POSSESSION

In parallel structure, parallel ideas are expressed in the same grammatical form. Therefore, in parallel construction the possessive form is carried through.

NO: His life is more burdensome than his wife.

YES: His life is more burdensome than his wife's.

NO: The pharmacist's work differs from the chemist.

YES: The pharmacist's work differs from the chemist's.

NO: Her dress, like Mrs. Jones, was low cut.

YES: Her dress, like Mrs. Jones', was low cut.

7. POSSESSIVE FOLLOWED BY AN APPOSITIVE

When a possessive is followed by an <u>appositive</u>, a word or group of words complementing or supplementing another, the "'s" is added to the appositive:

It was Jason the gardener's move.

I took Mrs. Green my teacher's advice.

My sister Mary's car runs well.

Her friend Christopher's dog always barks.

An appositive (or explanatory word or group of words) set off by commas implies that it is not essential to the meaning of the sentence. In such a case, the possessive may be formed on both the main noun and on the explanatory word or on only the explanatory word.

It was Jason's, the gardener's, move.
                OR
It was Jason, the gardener's, move.

I took Mrs. Green's, my teacher's, advice.

42

OR

I took Mrs. Green, my teacher's, advice.

My sister's, Mary's, car runs well.
OR
My sister, Mary's, car runs well.

Her friend's, Christopher's, dog always barks.
OR
Her friend, Christopher's, dog always barks.

8. POSSESSION WITH COMPOUND WORDS

Use the last word in a compound word to form the possessive even if the compound is not hyphenated.

Singular possessive	Plural	Plural possessive
mother-in-law's	*mothers-in-law*	*mothers-in-law's*
secretary general's	*secretaries general*	*secretaries general's*
chief executive officer's	*chief executive officers*	*chief executive officers'*
commander-in chief's	*commanders-in chief*	*commanders-in chief's*
notary public's	*notaries public*	*notaries public's*
Queen of England's	*Queens of England*	*Queens of England's*

With compounds, especially compound plurals, it is better to recast the sentence and use an "of" phrase than use the possessive form.

> *The mother-in-law's meeting...*
>
> *PREFER:*   *The meeting of the mother-in-law...*
>
> *The commanders-in-chiefs' advice...*
>
> *PREFER:*   *The advice of the commanders-in-chiefs...*
>
> *The notaries public's vote...*
>
> *PREFER:*   *The vote of the notaries public...*

9. POSSESSIVE USED ALONE

The possessive is sometimes used alone to indicate a place of business or a residence:

the doctor's	*the cleaner's*
the butcher's	*the shoemaker's*
the Smith's	*John and Sharon's*

10. DOUBLE POSSESSIVE

A double possessive, perfectly acceptable in English, uses both the 's and an "of" form.

friends of Mary's	*relatives of Mr. Green's*

2.8 EXERCISES

NOUNS

A. In the following sentences label the various nouns: proper noun (P); common noun (COM); concrete noun (CON); abstract noun (A) and collective noun (COL). Also make a note when the noun is noncountable (NC).

1. Linda celebrated Memorial Day at home this year.

2. John Keats wrote in his poem "Ode on a Grecian Urn," "Beauty is Truth."

3. Winter vacation begins this Monday.

4. We had our picnic by the lake.

5. In Plato's dialogue The Crito, the concept of justice is discussed.

6. The jury found the defendant guilty by reason of insanity.

7. There was so much dust on the furniture that I sneezed.

8. Supply and demand is a basic law of economics.

9. Both orchestras performed Handel's Messiah at the winter concert.

10. Reggie told us the good news while we were having coffee.

B. As indicated in the parentheses complete the following sentences with a suitable compound noun.

1. She brought the gum in a _____.(noun and noun)

2. Construction work is _____.(noun and gerund)

3. He visited the doctor for his annual _____. (noun and adverbial preposition)

4. They solved the problem through _____. (adjective and noun)

5. He paid the bill with a _____. (possessive noun and noun)

6. They entered the house with a _____. (verb and noun)

7. She served dinner in the _____. (gerund and noun)

8. The problem can be solved through _____. (noun, conjunction and noun)

9. The vegetables were _____. (preposition and noun)

2.8 EXERCISES

10. The building was completed after they were given the
    _____. (verb and adverbial preposition)

GENDER

Complete the following sentences with a noun as indicated
in the parentheses.

1. He gave the gift to his _____. (feminine)
2. He read the _____ to his _____. (neuter, common)
3. Ask _____ to tell me the time. (masculine)
4. His _____ is a famous _____. (feminine, common)
5. That _____ belonged to his _____. (neuter, common)

NUMBER

Change the following words to the plural form.

1. birch, _____
2. motto, _____
3. bay, _____
4. vertebra, _____
5. self, _____
6. sheriff, _____
7. appendix, _____
8. lady, _____
9. focus, _____
10. alto, _____
11. carry, _____
12. crisis, _____
13. fly, _____
14. relay, _____
15. idea, _____
16. basis, _____

2.8 EXERCISES

17. phenomenon , _____
18. ox _____
19. employ, _____
20. studio, _____
21. fifty, _____
22. deer, _____
23. symposium, _____
24. chief, _____
25. stomach, _____

POSSESSIVE CASE

A. Change the following nouns to the possessive case.

EXAMPLE: *The coat of Jane; Jane's coat.*

1. the observations of the witness, _____
2. the reference of the man, _____
3. the stand of the group, _____
4. to the surprise of everyone, _____
5. work of one week, _____
6. the texture of the sculpture, _____
7. the blouse of Melissa, _____
8. the tail of the fox, _____
9. the house of the grandparents, _____
10. a race of the horse, _____
11. the strike of the company, _____
12. the point of the scissors, _____
13. the choice of the boy, _____
14. the end of the month, _____
15. the worth of ten dollars, _____
16. the color of the car, _____
17. the production of this year, _____

2.8 EXERCISES

18. the dancer of the ballet, _____

19. the bud of the flower, _____

20. the failure of the play, _____

B. Make the necessary corrections in the following sentences.

1. His suit, like James, was grey.

2. The president's adviser's past was investigated.

3. The pitcher's job is more difficult than the fielders.

4. The woman's cat's kittens were given away.

5. The majority leader of the House of Representatives' speech was well received.

6. The final plans of the Boy Scouts of America's meeting were made.

7. It was Susan, Ann, Joan and my idea.

8. The amateurs' life differs from the professionals.

9. That is Dr. White and her new house.

10. The play's ending satisfied the audience.

11. It was Mark the presidents decision.

12. The bus driver's and train conductor's unions went on strike.

13. We are not allowed to use Mom's and Dad's car.

14. That is Jane's, the nurses, car.

15. Frank's and Mary's package arrived today.

CHAPTER 3

PRONOUNS

Pronouns are the simple, everyday words used to refer to people, places or things that have already been mentioned, such as _him_, _she_, _me_, _it_, or to indefinite people, places, things or qualities, such as _who_, _where_, _this_, or _somebody_. They usually replace some noun and make an expression concise. There are only about fifty pronouns in the English language and most are short words, however they can be difficult to use correctly. One reason these words may be so difficult to use properly is their frequency of occurrence. Of the twenty-five most commonly used words in the English language, ten are pronouns. Perhaps it. is due to their frequent usage that pronouns have acquired a variety of distinctive functions. Although pronouns are dissimilar in the ways they may or may not be used, they have two things in common. The first is their ability to stand alone, or "stand in" for nouns. The second is that they all have little specific meaning. Whatever meaning they have derives from the context in which they are found. Some pronouns that modify other words are also adjectives. In this chapter, we will mainly speak of pronouns that stand alone-- that take the place either of a definite noun or of an unknown or uncertain noun. Pronouns used as adjectives are discussed in the chapter "ADJECTIVES AND ADVERBS." When we use pronouns as adjectives in examples in this chapter, they are marked (a.).

> _Who_ are _you_ speaking to?
>
> _That_ is _my_ (a.) hat _you_ are holding in _your_ (a.) hand.
>
> _Marsha herself_ (a.) told _them all_ (a.) about _what_ happened to _her_ when _it_ started to rain.
>
> _Somebody_ had to let the _others_ know _that she_ was not to blame.
>
> _Who_, _what_, _where_, _when_, and _how_ are the five words by _which_ _you_ can organize _this_.

This is a new kind of information for *me* and *I* regret
to *some* (a.) degree *that* *I* can't be *more* in touch with
them.

She doesn't agree with *me*; *that's* too bad, but *that's*
the way *it* is.

I've had *enough*! If *no one* wants to take care of *it*, *I'll*
do *it* *myself* (a.).

It is not *enough* to think of *me*; *you* should send *me* a
letter *when* *you* do.

I wonder *what* is in *it*.

All the underlined words in the preceding sentences are
pronouns. Traditionally pronouns are divided into six
groups; each group has its own name, definition and special
functions. These categories are helpful in learning how to
recognize the different kinds of pronouns and how to use
them correctly, since they come in such a wide variety of
forms.

3.1 PERSONAL PRONOUNS

Because of their many forms, this can be a troublesome group:

CASE

NUMBER	PERSON	SUBJECT	OBJECT	POSSESSIVE	POSSESSIVE ADJECTIVE
Sing-ular	First person	*I*	*me*	*mine*	*my*
	2nd person	*you*	*you*	*yours*	*your*
	* 3rd person (masc.)	*he*	*him*	*his*	*his*
	(fem.)	*she*	*her*	*hers*	*her*
	(neuter)	*it*	*it*		*its*
Plural	First	*we*	*us*	*ours*	*our*
	Second	*you*	*you*	*yours*	*your*
	Third	*they*	*them*	*theirs*	*their*

_____ saw it.   Let _____ .   That's _____ . _____ house.

* When a pronoun is used to refer to someone (other than the speaker or the person spoken to), the "third person" is used, and a different form of the pronoun is employed to show the gender of the person referred to. *His, her, him, his,* and *hers,* all indicate the masculine or feminine gender. *It* and *its* refer to something to which gender does not apply.

There are three forms of personal pronouns:

1. PERSON: to indicate whether the person is the speaker (1st person), the person being spoken to (2nd person), or the person being spoken about (3rd person).

2. CASE: to show the job the pronoun is performing in the sentence.

3. NUMBER: to indicate whether the word is plural or singular.

EXAMPLES OF PERSONAL PRONOUN USE:

I went yesterday to see her.

You have my (a.) hat, don't you?

Her car was formerly theirs.

Between you and me, I really don't want to go with him.

In his opinion, the boating dock is ours, not yours.

They say you can't take it with you.

Won't you walk down to his garden with them?

Errors to Avoid--Pronoun Case

When a compound subject or object includes a pronoun, be sure that the case chosen is in agreement with the pronoun's place in the sentence--a subject case pronoun is used as the subject of the verb, an object case pronoun is used as the object, etc. The same rule of agreement is true when using an appositive (a word or words with the same meaning as the pronoun); the pronoun must be in the same case form as the word it renames.

Compounds:

Both Mary and he (NOT him) have seen that movie. (subject-- "Mary and he")

Last year the team elected both Jane and me (NOT I).

(object-- "Jane and me")

Could you wait for my brother and me (NOT I)?
(object of a preposition--"My brother and me")

A trip to Europe appealed to Susan and him (NOT he).
(object of a preposition--"Susan and him")

There has always been a great friendship between you
and me (NOT I).   (object of a preposition-- "You and
me")

Mrs. Williams and I (NOT me) will direct the chorus.
(subject-- "Mrs. Williams and I")

Appositions: words with the same meaning as the pronoun.

We Americans value freedom. (subject)

They invited us (NOT we) cheerleaders. (object)

Let's you and me (NOT I) go together.   (object)

Both players, James and he (NOT him), could be
stars. (subject)

Our school sent two delegates, Mark and him (NOT
he)..   (object)

It is not for we writers to determine editorial policy.
(subject)

Will you give your decision to us applicants soon?
(object)

3.2 RELATIVE PRONOUNS--Interior Sentences (Clauses)

Relative pronouns play the part of subject or object in
sentences within sentences (clauses). They often refer to
nouns that have preceded them, making the sentence more
compact.

> *NO: The flower--the flower was yellow-- made her*
>   *smile.*
> *YES: The flower, which was yellow, made her smile.*
>
> *NO: The girl--the girl lived down the block-- loved*
>   *him.*

YES: The girl <u>who</u> lived down the block loved him.

Sometimes their reference is indefinite:

> *I wonder <u>what</u> happened.* (The event that occurred is uncertain.)

> *I'll call <u>whomever</u> you want.* (The people to be called are unknown.)

<u>Who</u> (for persons), <u>that</u> (for persons and things), and <u>which</u> (for things), are the most common pronouns of this type.

<u>Who</u> can cause problems because it changes form depending on the part it plays in the interior sentence (clause):

> <u>Subject</u>   <u>Object</u>   <u>Possessive</u>
>
> *who*   *whom*   *whose*

> *Mr. Jackson, <u>whom</u> I know well, called yesterday. (object)*

> *Mr. Jackson, <u>who</u> is my friend, called yesterday. (subject)*

> *Mr. Jackson, <u>whose</u> friendship is important to me, called yesterday.*

3.3 INTERROGATIVE PRONOUNS-- Questions

These pronouns are easy to recognize because they always introduce either direct or indirect questions. The words just discussed as relative pronouns are called <u>interrogative pronouns</u> when they introduce a question: <u>who</u>, <u>what</u>, <u>that</u>, <u>which</u>, <u>whom</u>, <u>whose</u>, <u>whoever</u>, <u>whichever</u>, and <u>whatever</u>.

> <u>Who</u> *is at the door? (refers to a person)*

> <u>What</u> *do you want from me? (refers to a thing)*

> <u>Which</u> *(flavor) do you want?*   *(refers to a thing*
> <u>Which</u> *(a.) boy won the match?*   *or person)*

> <u>Whatever</u> *you mean by "liberal education," I don't know.*

Is that what you meant to say?

Whom did you telephone last night?

Sometimes an interrogative is not recognized when it is used indirectly inside another sentence:

She wondered who was at the door.

Samuel asked them what they wanted.

He didn't know if he would ever find out what happened.

I couldn't guess which they would choose.

3.4 DEMONSTRATIVE PRONOUNS-- Pointers

This, *that*, *these*, and *those* are the most common words used as pronouns to point to someone or something clearly expressed or implied:

That is the apple I wanted. (subject)

Bring me those, please. (object)

I must tell him that. (object)

These are the ones I've been looking for. (subject)

That really made me mad! (subject)

"This above all, to thine own self be true." (subject)

Give this to her for me. (object)

Such or *so* may also serve as pointing pronouns:

Such was his fate. (subject)

He resented Jerry and told him so. (object)

These same words are often used as adjectives and at first glance it is easy to classify them only as adjectives, forgetting that they also take the place of nouns and serve as pronouns.

That apple is the one I want. (adjective describing "apple")

Bring me <u>those</u> books, please. (adjective describing
  "books")

I must tell him <u>that</u> story. (adjective describing "story")

It was <u>such</u> a tiring day. (adjective describing "day")

She was <u>so</u> happy. (adjective describing "happy")

3.5 INDEFINITE PRONOUNS

This group of pronouns acquired its name because the reference
(the noun for which they are standing in) is indefinite.

<u>Indefinite persons or things</u>: (all singular pronouns)

everybody	*everyone*
somebody	*someone*
anybody	*anyone*
nobody	*no one*

<u>Everybody</u> joined in the chorus.

<u>No one</u> took less than he did.

Is <u>anyone</u> here?

I hope <u>someone</u> answers my calls.

<u>Indefinite quantities</u>:

each		*either*
another	*all*	*some*
several	*both*	*few*
least	*less*	*little*
lots	*many*	*plenty*
other	*most*	*more*

<u>Much</u> has been said on the subject of delinquency.

She took <u>several</u> for herself.

It is <u>less</u> than I'd bargained for.

Dallas or Houston-- <u>either</u> would be fine for me.

There are <u>plenty</u> of people who want your job.

<u>Many</u> are called, but few are chosen.

The <u>most</u> we can expect is to see her next week.

<u>Each</u> must chart his own course.

The biggest problem encountered with these pronouns is in trying to decide if they are singular or plural. See "AGREE-MENT" for a discussion of this problem.

3.6 REFLEXIVE PRONOUNS

These are the pronouns that end in *<u>"self"</u>* or *<u>"selves"</u>*.

myself	*yourself*	*yourselves*
himself	*herself*	*itself*
ourselves	*themselves*	

Their main purpose is to reflect back on the subject of a sentence:

She cut <u>herself</u>. (object, refers to "she")

I bought <u>myself</u> a new dress. (object, refers to "I")

You are just not <u>yourself</u> today. (object, refers to "you")

They consider <u>themselves</u> lucky. (object, refers to "they")

Give <u>yourself</u> a treat; go to the ice cream shop. (object, refers to "you" understood)

After that dust storm I washed <u>myself</u> vey well. (object, refers to "I")

They also provide emphasis. When they serve this purpose, they appear either right after the subject or at the end of the sentence.

We <u>ourselves</u> will triumph over this outrage.

I <u>myself</u> will go to the ticket office.

She will tell it to him <u>herself</u>.

You yourself must discover the meaning.

I suppose I will have to do it myself.

Errors to Avoid--Reflexive Pronouns

Do not use the reflexive in place of the shorter personal pronoun:

> *NO: Both Sandy and myself plan to go.*
> *YES: Both Sandy and I plan to go.*

> *NO: Yourself will take on the challenges of college.*
> *YES: You will take on the challenges of college.*

> *NO: Either James or yourself will paint the mural.*
> *YES: Either James or you will paint the mural.*

Watch out for careless use of the pronoun form:

> *NO: George hisself told me it was true.*
> *YES: George himself told me it was true.*

> *NO: They washed the car theirselves.*
> *YES: They washed the car themselves.*

Notice that the reflexive pronouns are not set off by commas:

> *NO: Mary, herself, gave him the diploma.*
> *YES: Mary herself gave him the diploma.*

> *NO: I will do it, myself.*
> *YES: I will do it myself.*

3.7 CASE--The Function of the Pronoun in a Sentence

By far the pronouns with which we are apt to make the most mistakes are those that change their form when they play different parts in a sentence -- the personal pronouns and the relative pronoun *who*. A careful study of the peculiarities of these changes is necessary to avoid the mistakes associated with their use.

3.7.1 SUBJECT CASE--(used mainly when the pronoun is a subject)

Use the subject case (*I*, *we*, *you*, *he*, *she*, *it*, *they*, *who*, and *whoever*) for the following purposes:

1. As a subject or a repeated subject:

> *NO: Mrs. Jones and me left early yesterday.*
>
> *YES: Mrs. Jones and I left early yesterday.*
>
> *NO: I know whom that is.*
>
> *YES: I know who that is. (subject of "is")*
>
> *NO: Us girls always go out together.*
>
> *YES: We girls always go out together.*
>
> *("girls" is the subject, "we" repeats it)*

Watch out for a parenthetical expression (an expression that is not central to the meaning of the sentence). It looks like a subject and verb when actually it is the pronoun that is the subject:

> *NO: Larry is the one whom we know will do the best job.*
>
> *YES: Larry is the one who we know will do the best job.*
> (Do not be misled by "we know"; who is the subject of the verb "will do".)
>
> *NO: It was Jim and Gretchen whom I think were there.*
>
> *YES: It was Jim and Gretchen who I think were there.*
> (Disregard "I think", who is the subject of were.)

2. Following the verb "to be" when it has a subject:
This is a part of the language that appears to be changing. It is a good example of how the grammar of a language follows speech and not the other way around. The traditional guideline has been that a pronoun following a form of "be" must be in the same case as the word before the verb.

> *It is I.* ("It" is the subject.)
>
> *I thought it was she.* ("it" is the subject.)
>
> *Was it they who arrived late?* ("it" is the subject.)

Our ear tells us that in informal conversation "It is I" would sound too formal, so instead we tend to say:

> *It is me. (in conversation)*
>
> *I thought it was her. (in conversation)*
>
> *Was it them who arrived late? (in conversation)*

In written English, however, it is best to follow the standard of using the subject case after the verb "be" when "be" is preceded by a word in the subject case, even though the pronoun is in the position of an object.

Some more examples that might cause trouble:

> *NO: Last week, the best students were you and me.*
>
> *YES: Last week, the best students were you and I. (refers to "students", subject of "were")*
>
> *NO: Whenever I hear that knock, I know it must be him.*
>
> *YES: Whenever I hear that knock, I know it must be he. (refers to "it", subject of "must be")*
>
> *NO: The leaders of the parade were John, Susan and me.*
>
> *YES: The leaders of the parade were John, Susan and I. (refers to "leaders", subject of "were")*
>
> *NO: I am expecting my mother to call. Is that her?*
>
> *YES: I am expecting my mother to call. Is that she? (refers to "mother", subject of "to call")*

3. As a subject when the verb is omitted (often after *than* or *as*):

> *I have known her longer than he. ("has known her" is understood)*
>
> *She sings as well as I. ("sing" is understood)*
>
> *We do just as well in algebra as they. ("do" is understood)*
>
> *He is much better than I at such calculations. ("than I am at such calculations"--"am" is understood)*

To test whether the subject or the object form is correct, complete the phrase in your mind and it will be obvious.

3.7.2 OBJECT CASE--(used mainly when the pronoun is an object)

Use the <u>object case</u> (*me*, *us*, *him*, *her*, *it*, *you*, *them*, *whom*, *whomever*) as follows:

1. <u>As the direct or indirect object, object of a preposition, or repeated object</u>:

> *The postman gave <u>me</u> the letter.* (indirect object)
>
> *Mr. Boone appointed <u>him</u> and <u>me</u> to clean the room.* ("him and me" is the object of "appointed")
>
> *They told <u>us</u> managers to rewrite the first report.* ("managers" is the indirect object of "told"; "us" repeats)
>
> *My attorney gave <u>me</u> a letter giving <u>her</u> power of attorney.* ("me" is the indirect object of "gave"; "her" is the indirect object of "giving")
>
> *That package is from <u>me</u>.* (object of "from")
>
> *Between <u>you</u> and <u>me</u>, I'm voting Republican.* (object of "between")
>
> <u>Whom</u> *were you thinking about?* (object of "about")
>
> *I know <u>whom</u> you asked.* (object of "asked")
>
> *My teacher gave both of <u>us</u>, June and <u>me</u>, an 'A'.* ("us" is the object of "of"; "June and me" repeats the object)

2. <u>As the subject of an infinitive verb</u>:

> *I wanted <u>her</u> to come.*
>
> *Janet invited <u>him and me</u> to attend the conference.*
>
> *He asked <u>her</u> to duplicate the report for the class.*
>
> <u>Whom</u> *will we ask to lead the group?* ("Whom" is the subject of "to lead")

3. <u>As an object when the verb or preposition is omitted</u>:

> *Father told my sister June more about it than (he told) <u>me</u>.*
>
> *The telephone calls were more often for Marilyn than (they were for) <u>him</u>.*
>
> *Did they send them as much candy as (they sent) <u>us</u>?*

He always gave Susan more than (he gave) me.

4. <u>Following "to be"</u>:

In point number 2, we learned that the subject of an infinitive verb form must be in the object case. The infinitive "to be" is an exception to this rule. Forms of "to be" must have the same case before and after the verb. If the word preceding the verb is in the subject case, the pronoun following must be in the subject case also. (Ex: <u>It</u> is <u>I</u>.) If the word before the verb is an object, the pronoun following must be objective as well.

We thought the <u>author</u> of the note to be <u>her</u>.

You expected the <u>winner</u> to be <u>me</u>.

Mother did not guess <u>it</u> to be Julie and <u>me</u> at the door.

Had you assumed the <u>experts</u> to be <u>us</u>?

5. <u>Subject of a progressive verb form</u> that functions as an <u>adjective (participle--"ing" ending)</u>:

Two kinds of words commonly end in "ing": a <u>participle</u>, or a word that looks like a verb but acts like an <u>adjective</u>, and a <u>gerund</u>, a word that looks like a verb but acts like a noun. When an "ing" word acts like an adjective, its subject is in the object case.

<u>For example</u>:

Can you imagine <u>him</u> <u>acting</u> that way? ("acting" refers to the pronoun and is therefore a participle which takes a subject in the object case, "him")

They watched <u>me</u> <u>smiling</u> at all the visitors. ("smiling" refers to the pronoun, which must be objective, "me")

<u>Compare</u>:

Can you imagine <u>his</u> <u>acting</u> in that part? (Here the emphasis is on "acting"; "his" refers to "acting" which is functioning as a noun (it is a <u>gerund</u>) and takes the possessive case.)

It was <u>my</u> <u>smiling</u> that won the contest. (Emphasis is on "smiling"--it is playing the part of a noun and so takes a possessive case pronoun "my")

3.7.3 POSSESSIVE CASE

Use the possessive adjective case (*my*, *our*, *your*, *her*, *his*, *its*, *their*, *whose*) in the following situations:

1. To indicate possession, classification of something, or connection. Possession is the most common:

> *I borrowed her car.* (*The car belongs to her.*)
>
> *Come over to our house.* (*The house belongs to us.*)
>
> *That is Jane's and my report .* (*The report belongs to us.*)
>
> *It is anyone's guess.*
>
> *Whose coat is this?*
>
> *The plant needs water; its leaves are fading.*

2. Preceding a verb acting as a noun (gerund):

> *Our leaving early helped end the party.*
>
> *Whose testifying will you believe?*
>
> *His reading was excessive.*
>
> *Don't you think her playing astounded them?*

Since there are no possessive forms for the demonstrative pronouns *that*, *this*, *these*, and *those*, they do not change form before a gerund:

> *NO: What are the chances of that's being painted today?*
>
> *YES: What are the chances of that being painted today?*

Use the possessive case (*mine*, *ours*, *yours*, *hers*, *his*, *its*, *theirs*, *whose*) in the following situations:

In any role a noun might play--a subject, object or complement with a possessive meaning.

> *Hers was an exciting career.* ("Hers" is the subject of "was")
>
> *Can you tell me whose this is?* ("whose" is the complement of "is")
>
> *He is a friend of mine.* ("mine" is the object of the preposition "of")
>
> *We borrowed theirs last week; it is only right that they should use ours this week.* ("theirs" is the object of

the verb "borrowed"; "ours" is the object of the verb "use")

I thought that was Mary's and his. ("Mary's and his" is the complement of the verb "was")

IT AND THERE—EXPLETIVES

Dictionaries will tell you that *it* and *there* are pronouns, but they are somewhat different from pronouns. They have even less meaning than the sometimes vague or indefinite pronouns. Because they provide so little information, their sole function is to fill space, to provide a formal subject for a sentence.

IT—IMPERSONAL

It's cold outside. (what is "it"?)

It's March 3.

What is this? It's my comb.

It's ten after three.

It's a twenty-minute walk to the grocery store.

It seems warmer than yesterday.

I know it gets crowded here at noon.

IT—ANTICIPATORY

Sometimes *it* fills the subject position while the actual subject appears later in the sentence. The underlined sections of the following sentences are the actual subjects.

It's surprising how handsome he is.

It's interesting to know your background.

It's curious that Mary paints so well.

It's hard to keep reading this.

It's pleasant to study words.

It's good knowing you are waiting for me.

Notice how *there* has no meaning but only fills the space of the subject:

There are three of us watching you.

There is lightning outside.

There are many ways to peel an onion.

There are only a few teachers who teach well.

There's a sale at Gimbel's.

There shall come a time when all this will end.

There is also often used as an adverb. If *there* is an expletive (space-filler), it is likely to be accompanied by "a". If it is accompanied by "the", it is probably an adverb and not a space-filler.

There's a place I'd like to visit. (space-filler)

There's the place I'd like to visit. (adverb referring to "is")

There's a girl in the corner. (space-filler)

There's the girl in the corner. (adverb referring to "is")

Agreement between the pronoun and the word(s) it refers to:

A pronoun usually takes the place of some noun. The noun (or group of words that works as a noun) for which the pronoun stands in is called the antecedent. It usually comes before the pronoun in the sentence or the paragraph. It is important to remember that the pronoun and the word(s) it refers to have to "agree". If the antecedent is plural, the pronoun should be plural; if the antecedent is singular, the pronoun must also be. The gender and person must also be consistent.

I heard one dog barking his loudest.

I heard three dogs barking their loudest.

The woman raised her hand.

The children raised their hands.

The man read his newspaper.

3.8 EXERCISES

A. <u>RELATIVE PRONOUNS</u> -- Complete the following sentences with a relative pronoun.

1. The man, _____ is standing in line, is a famous author.

2. She looks sad. I wonder _____ news she received.

3. The house, _____ was white, has been abandoned.

4. _____ one you chose will satisfy me.

5. I'll sing _____ you want.

6. The dress, _____ I borrowed from Mary, was lost in the cleaners.

7. The only seat _____ is available is the corner one.

B. <u>RELATIVE PRONOUNS</u> -- "Who and Whom". In the following sentences choose the correct form of the pronoun given in the parentheses.

1. It's Susan from (*who, whom*) I received the assignment.

2. I must see the teacher (*who, whom*) I spoke with last week.

3. She is a girl (*who, whom*) I know very well.

4. I can't remember (*who, whom*) I met yesterday.

5. If you know (*who, whom*) sent the letter, please give me a name and an address.

6. This book will go to (*whoever, whomever*) lost it.

7. John (*who, whom*) played the lead in the play, was a great success.

8. When they know (*who, whom*) won the election, let me know.

9. The club is entitled to choose (*whoever, whomever*) they want for President.

10. Was it he (*who, whom*) won the race?

3.8 EXERCISES

C. <u>INTERROGATIVE AND DEMONSTRATIVE PRONOUNS</u> -- Write five sentences using different interrogative pronouns. Then do the same exercise for demonstrative pronouns. In some of your sentences try using the pronouns in their less common role. Use them indirectly inside a sentence (interrogative pronoun), and as adjectives (demonstrative pronoun).

D. <u>REFLEXIVE PRONOUNS</u> -- Complete the following sentences with the appropriate reflexive pronoun. Also note which pronoun the "reflector" is an object of.

1. We found _____ out of money.

2. I _____ will complete the project.

3. Give _____ the time needed.

4. The play, by_____, was quite good.

5. They will give it to him _____.

E. <u>REFLEXIVE PRONOUNS</u> -- In the following sentences, make the necessary corrections.

1. Both James and themselves went to the beach.

2. Jack, himself, read the speech.

3. Myself will unload the car.

4. They finished the painting theirselves.

5. He mowed the lawn, hisself.

F. <u>PERSONAL PRONOUNS</u> -- In the following sentences choose the correct form of the pronoun given in the parentheses.

1. Both Peter and (*I, me*) went to the movies.

2. They missed the train because of (*he, him*).

3. (*We, Us*) soldiers must be ready for combat at all times.

4. You and (*I, me*) have always understood each other.

5. I don't know if it was (*she, her*) who was in the theater yesterday.

3.8 EXERCISES

6. Susan and *(he, him)* have met before.

7. Neither Jack nor *(they, them)* will be going on vacation this summer.

8. We sing just as well as *(they, them)*.

9. Do *(we, us)* officers have to attend the convention?

10. I am older than *(she, her)*.

11. Mr. Grey and *(I, me)* will paint the scenery for the play.

12. Paul questioned *(she, her)* and *(I, me)* about the accident.

13. Both students, Mark and *(he, him)* were suspended from school.

14. They told *(us, we)* to clean the house.

15. Was it *(they, them)* who stopped by yesterday afternoon?

16. Sometimes *(we, us)* voters feel powerless.

17. I believed the winner of the contest to be *(he, him)*.

18. Boys like *(they, them)* could never make the football team.

19. Can you believe *(I, me)* doing that well?

20. Give *(we, us)* beginners a chance!

21. You expected the performer to be *(he, him)*.

22. Did you receive as much as *(me, I)*?

23. It appears that Joan and *(they, them)* have left the club.

24. They selected *(we, us)* musicians.

25. They asked *(he, him)* to drive.

26. Joe and *(I, me)* attend every school concert.

27. I can't believe you selected Sylvia and *(she, her)*.

28. Neither you nor *(I, me)* can wait till spring arrives.

3.8 EXERCISES

G.   Complete the following sentences with an appropriate possessive pronoun.

1. _____ car is this?

2. That is _____ dress in the closet.

3. What are the chances of _____ being finished tomorrow?

4. _____ intelligence was staggering.

5. They are relatives of _____.

6. _____ was a beautiful house.

7. We didn't know that was James' and _____.

H.   Complete the following sentences with the correct expletive.

1. _____the first day of March.

2. _____ are only a few chances left.

3. _____ time to finish the game.

4. _____looks like rain.

5. _____ interesting to read history.

I.   Complete the following sentences with an appropriate pronoun.

1. The girl picked up _____ books.

2. The detectives finished _____ case.

3. I saw a beaver building _____ nest.

4. The villagers had _____ meetings on Wednesdays.

5. John left _____ key at home.

CHAPTER 4

VERBS

Every sentence must have a verb. Verbs express action or a state of being. Small changes in their form reflect many differences in meaning. One variable is number; a verb can be either singular or plural:

> I <u>am</u> happy to be here. *(singular)*
> We <u>are</u> not so sure of the date. *(plural)*

> Jill <u>loves</u> chocolate chip cookies. *(singular)*
> Mother and father <u>love</u> to go sailing. *(plural)*

> The baby <u>has</u> a cold. *(singular)*
> They <u>have</u> four horses in the country. *(plural)*

Verbs are also distinguished by person: first (I, we), second (you), and third (he, she, it, they, one). Usually, verbs change form only in the third person singular.

> I, you, we, they <u>hope</u> you will stay.
> He, she, <u>hopes</u> you will leave.

> I, you, we, they <u>grow</u>.
> He, she, it, one <u>grows</u>.

Changes made in the forms of words in order to indicate slight changes of meaning are called <u>inflections</u>. Verbs change more readily and more often than any other sort of word, and because of this can often be confusing. Through hearing English spoken, and learning to speak it yourself, you have probably learned the rules and peculiarities associated with correct verb usage without even thinking about it; you know when something "sounds right" that it probably is. But there are rules and logic which explain why some things "sound right" and others don't. When something sounds wrong to your ear, it is probably due to a mistake in either tense, irregular verb useage, or agreement.

4.1 TENSE

Tense means time. Verbs have the ability to tell us not only what action is occurring, but also when it is occurring. The form of a verb changes to indicate when an action takes place. The two main forms of any verb are the present and the past tense. The past tense is usually formed by adding _-ed_ to the basic verb.

PRESENT	PAST
walk	_walked_
talk	_talked_
smoke	_smoked_
look	_looked_
listen	_listened_
finish	_finished_
telephone	_telephoned_
help	_helped_
prove	_proved_
enter	_entered_

Verbs that follow this pattern in forming the past tense are called regular verbs. Almost all of the verbs in the language are regular. Yet, there are about 100 commonly used verbs that do not follow this pattern. These are known as irregular verbs, and will be discussed in more detail later on in the chapter.

Although the past and present are the only form changes in single word verbs, there are certain verb phrases that are also used with the verbs to indicate changes in time. When these verb phrases are added to the past and present tenses, there are actually six tenses in the English language:

Present: present time, action or condition going on now _(yawn, am yawning)_.

Past: past time, action is completed _(yawned)_.

Future: future time, action or condition is expected to happen or come _(will yawn, shall yawn)_.

Present Perfect: action occurred in the past and is complete in the present *(have (has) yawned)*.

Past Perfect: past action completed before another past action *(had yawned)*.

Future Perfect: future action to be completed before another future action *(will have yawned)*.

As you can see, some of these tenses make it possible to express quite subtle variations in time. The three perfect tenses as well as the future tense are formed by adding a helping or auxiliary verb to the past participle, which is usually formed by adding -ed to the main verb. The perfect tenses show that an action has been completed (perfected).

All six of the main tenses also have a companion form: the progressive form. This can also be considered a tense, as it shows that action is in progress. Progressive forms are expressed with some form of the verb to be and the ending -ing added to the main verb. Examples:

He is looking at the birds. (present progressive)

They were looking at the mirror. (past progressive)

He will be looking for her tomorrow. (future progressive)

I have been looking at the tree. (present perfect progressive)

We had been looking for a house. (past perfect progressive)

She will have been looking for the right material for her drapes for three years. (future perfect progressive)

It is not necessary to learn the names of all these tenses; they are introduced only so that you may have some familiarity with the terms and a better understanding of the logic behind the language. The most important parts of the study of verb forms for an English-speaking student are the study of common errors and practice using the correct forms.

The verbs that are apt to cause the most trouble are the irregular verbs, because it is easy to confuse the past tense and the past participle.

He drank (not drunk) his fill of beer.

After he had eaten (not ate) his dinner, he left.

I had gone (not went) down to see Jim.

He began (not begun) his day early.

To review, the regular verbs form the past tense by adding -d or -ed to the present tense of the verb. The irregular verbs form the past tense in a number of different ways; there are no rules governing the formation of the past tense and past participles. They have to be studied and learned. Review the following list of commonly used irregular verbs to find the ones that most often cause you trouble.

4.1.1 MAIN PARTS OF COMMONLY USED IRREGULAR VERBS

PRESENT TENSE	PAST TENSE	PAST PARTICIPLE
am	was	been
arise	arose	arisen
attack	attacked	attacked
awake	awoke, awaked	awakened
bear	bore	born
beat	beat	beaten
become	became	become
begin	began	begun
bend	bent	bent
bind	bound	bound
bite	bit	bitten
bleed	bled	bled
blow	blew	blown
break	broke	broken
bring	brought	brought
build	built	built
burn	burned, burnt	burned, burnt
burst	burst	burst

PRESENT TENSE	PAST TENSE	PAST PARTICIPLE
buy	bought	bought
cast	cast	cast
choose	chose	chosen
climb	climbed	climbed
cling	clung	clung
come	came	come
creep	crept	crept
deal	dealt	dealt
dig	dug	dug
dive	dived, dove	dived
do	did	done
drag	dragged	dragged
draw	drew	drawn
dream	dreamed, dreamt	dreamed, dreamt
drink	drank	drunk
drive	drove	driven
drown	drowned	drowned
eat	ate	eaten
fall	fell	fallen
fight	fought	fought
find	found	found
flee	fled	fled
fling	flung	flung
flow	flowed	flowed
fly	flew	flown
forget	forgot	forgotten
forgive	forgave	forgiven
freeze	froze	frozen
get	got	got, gotten
give	gave	given
go	went	gone
grind	ground	ground

PRESENT TENSE	PAST TENSE	PAST PARTICIPLE
grow	grew	grown
hang (a picture)	hung	hung
hang (a person)	hanged	hanged
hear	heard	heard
heat	heated	heated
hide	hid	hidden
hit	hit	hit
hold	held	held
hurt	hurt	hurt
kneel	knelt	knelt
know	knew	known
lay (to place)	laid	laid
lead	led	led
leave	left	left
lend	lent	lent
lie (to rest)	lay	lain
lie (to tell a lie)	lied	lied
light	lighted, lit	lighted, lit
lose	lost	lost
make	made	made
mean	meant	meant
meet	met	met
mistake	mistook	mistaken
pay	paid	paid
prove	proved	proved, proven
put	put	put
read	read	read
rid	rid	rid
ride	rode	ridden
ring	rang	rung
rise	rose	risen
run	ran	run
say	said	said

PRESENT TENSE	PAST TENSE	PAST PARTICIPLE
see	saw	seen
seek	sought	sought
sell	sold	sold
send	sent	sent
set	set	set
sew	sewed	sewed, sewn
shake	shook	shaken
shine	shone	shone
show	showed	showed, shown
shrink	shrank	shrunk
sing	sang	sung
sit	sat	sat
slay	slew	slain
sleep	slept	slept
slide	slid	slid
speak	spoke	spoken
spend	spent	spent
spit	spit, spat	spit, spat
spring	sprang	sprung
steal	stole	stolen
sting	stung	stung
strike	struck	struck
strive	strive	striven
swear	swore	sworn
sweep	swept	swept
swim	swam	swum
swing	swung	swung
take	took	taken
teach	taught	taught
tear	tore	torn
tell	told	told
throw	threw	thrown
thrust	thrust	thrust

PRESENT TENSE	PAST TENSE	PAST PARTICIPLE
wake	waked, woke	waked, woken
wear	wore	worn
weave	wove	woven
weep	wept	wept
wind	wound	wound
wring	wrung	wrung
write	wrote	written

4.1.2 ERRORS TO AVOID IN TENSE OF VERBS

DO NOT CONFUSE THE PAST PARTICIPLE FOR THE PAST TENSE:

NO: *I swum two miles last week.*

YES: *I swam two miles last week.*

NO: *My shirt shrunk in the wash.*

YES: *My shirt shrank in the wash.*

NO: *We seen a lot of birds in the corn field.*

YES: *We saw a lot of birds in the corn field.*

NO: *Mari run all the way to town.*

YES: *Mari ran all the way to town.*

NO: *She sung so beautifully.*

YES: *She sang so beautifully.*

NO: *The grass sprung up really fast last spring.*

YES: *The grass sprang up really fast last spring.*

NO: *It begun to get dark early.*

YES: *It began to get dark early.*

NO: *Suddenly it come to me.*

YES: *Suddenly it came to me.*

LEARN THE IRREGULAR VERBS. DO NOT ADD REGULAR ENDINGS TO IRREGULAR VERB STEMS.

NO: *She arised late on Tuesday.*

YES: *She <u>arose</u> late on Tuesday.*

NO: *The bee <u>stinged</u> her.*
YES: *The bee <u>stung</u> her.*

NO: *I <u>sweared</u> to keep the secret.*
YES: *I <u>swore</u> to keep the secret.*

NO: *The batter <u>swinged</u> at the ball.*
YES: *The batter <u>swung</u> at the ball.*

NO: *Jack <u>weeped</u> when he heard the news.*
YES: *Jack <u>wept</u> when he heard the news.*

NO: *He <u>throwed</u> her the keys.*
YES: *He <u>threw</u> her the keys.*

NO: *The phone <u>ringed</u> twice.*
YES: *The phone <u>rang</u> twice.*

NO: *Susan <u>sleeped</u> peacefully.*
YES: *Susan <u>slept</u> peacefully.*

NO: *Do you know how much he <u>stealed</u>?*
YES: *Do you know how much he <u>stole</u>?*

DO NOT USE THE PRESENT FOR THE PAST TENSE:

NO: *Yesterday, he <u>sees</u> her twice.*
YES: *Yesterday, he <u>saw</u> her twice.*

NO: *Monday, I <u>says</u> to my sister, "Count me out."*
YES: *Monday, I <u>said</u> to my sister, "Count me out."*

NO: *Last night, he <u>finds</u> her alone with his friend.*
YES: *Last night, he <u>found</u> her alone with his friend.*

NO: *Last week, I <u>get</u> picked up twice for jaywalking.*
YES: *Last week, I <u>got</u> picked up twice for jaywalking.*

DO NOT USE THE PRESENT FOR THE FUTURE TENSE:

NO: *Next year I <u>go</u> to Germany to find work.*

YES: *Next year I <u>shall go</u> to Germany to find work.*

NO: *Tomorrow I <u>drive</u> into town.*

YES: *Tomorrow <u>I shall</u> drive into town.*

NO: *Next week she <u>begins</u> her studies.*

YES: *Next week she <u>will begin</u> her studies.*

NO: *We <u>come</u> to your house next Friday.*

YES: *We <u>shall come</u> to your house next Friday.*

DO NOT USE PAST FOR PAST PERFECT:

NO: *John asked whether I <u>ate</u> all my dinner.*

YES: *John asked whether I <u>had eaten</u> all my dinner.*

NO: *The dog attacked the cat after she <u>scratched</u> him.*

YES: *The dog attacked the cat after she <u>had scratched</u> him.*

NO: *Before mother arrived I <u>wrote</u> my paper.*

YES: *Before mother arrived I <u>had written</u> my paper.*

NO: *Before they got to the summit, the dam <u>burst</u>.*

YES: *Before they got to the summit, the dam <u>had burst</u>.*

DO NOT CONFUSE THE PAST TENSE FOR THE PAST
PARTICIPLE. ONLY THE PAST PARTICIPLE USES HELPING
VERBS:

NO: *He must have already <u>broke</u> the door.*

YES: *He must have already <u>broken</u> the door.*

NO: *They had <u>began</u> early.*

YES: *They had <u>begun</u> early.*

NO: *She has <u>wore</u> that dress hundreds of times.*

YES: *She has <u>worn</u> that dress hundreds of times.*

NO: *He had <u>swam</u> long enough.*

YES: *He had <u>swum</u> long enough.*

NO: *We had <u>rang</u> the doorbell many times.*

YES: *We had <u>rung</u> the doorbell many times.*

DO NOT SHIFT FROM THE PRESENT TO THE PAST IN THE SAME PHRASE:

NO: *The boy is raking the leaves and went for the basket.*

YES: *The boy is raking the leaves and goes for the basket.*

NO: *She writes slowly and rose to answer the phone.*

YES: *She writes slowly and rises to answer the phone.*

NO: *He runs into the room and shouted, "Here I am."*

YES: *He runs into the room and shouts, "Here I am."*

NO: *The baby is crawling on the floor and looked up at her mother.*

YES: *The baby is crawling on the floor and looks up at her mother.*

DO NOT SHIFT FROM THE PAST TO THE PRESENT IN THE SAME PHRASE:

NO: *She sat at the window and looks out.*

YES: *She sat at the window and looked out.*

NO: *We left quickly and trip on the step.*

YES: *We left quickly and tripped on the step.*

NO: *Mary forgot the letter and runs back for it.*

YES: *Mary forgot the letter and ran back for it.*

NO: *He came late and says he was sorry.*

YES: *He came late and said he was sorry.*

DO NOT CONFUSE SIMILAR VERBS. TWO PAIRS OF VERBS THAT OFTEN CAUSE TROUBLE ARE LIE AND LAY AND SIT AND SET:

Present	Past	Past Participle	"ing" Form
Lie (to rest)	*lay*	*lain*	*lying*
Lay (to place)	*laid*	*laid*	*laying*
Sit (to be seated)	*sat*	*sat*	*sitting*
Set (to place)	*set*	*set*	*setting*

LAY AND SET ALWAYS TAKE AN OBJECT SINCE THEY REFER TO SOMETHING. LIE AND SIT STAND ALONE.

NO: *Lay down here and rest.*

YES: *Lie down here and rest.*

NO: *The pen is laying on the table.*

YES: *The pen is lying on the table.*

NO: *I had laid down for a nap.*

YES: *I had lain down for a nap.*

NO: *The dog was setting there.*

YES: *The dog was sitting there.*

NO: *She sat it down on the floor.*

YES: *She set it down on the floor.*

4.2 AGREEMENT

When parts of a sentence agree, there is a logical relationship between them. The most important kind of agreement is between the subject and the verb. The verb must agree with the subject in both number and person. That is, if the subject is singular, the verb must also be; if the subject is plural, the verb must be plural. If the subject is in the third person (he, she, it, they, one), the verb must also be in the third person. The main difficulty is identifying the subject of the sentence and determining whether it is singular or plural. (For a discussion of how to recognize singular and plural subjects, see the chapter on nouns and pronouns.)

4.2.1 ERRORS TO AVOID IN AGREEMENT

DO NOT BE DISTRACTED BY WORDS THAT COME BETWEEN THE SUBJECT AND THE VERB. REMEMBER TO ALWAYS MAKE THE VERB AGREE WITH THE SUBJECT OF THE SENTENCE.

NO: *The arrival of many friends promise good times.*

YES: *The <u>arrival</u> of many friends <u>promises</u> good times.*

NO: *<u>All</u> the democrats including John <u>hopes</u> Murray wins.*

YES: *<u>All</u> the democrats including John <u>hope</u> Murray wins.*

NO: *Every <u>one</u> of you <u>know</u> your subject well.*

YES: *Every <u>one</u> of you <u>knows</u> your subject well.*

NO: *<u>Mary</u>, as well as the Joneses, <u>are</u> coming along.*

YES: *<u>Mary</u>, as well as the Joneses, <u>is</u> coming along.*

NO: *<u>Mr. Green</u>, along with Miss Oakley and Mr. Smith, <u>were</u> late.*

YES: *<u>Mr. Green</u>, along with Miss Oakley and Mr. Smith, <u>was</u> late.*

NO: *A <u>color</u> of many hues <u>are</u> most interesting.*

YES: *A <u>color</u> of many hues <u>is</u> most interesting.*

NO: *The <u>elm</u>, like most trees here, <u>turn</u> color in the fall.*

YES: *The <u>elm</u>, like most trees here, <u>turns</u> color in the fall.*

NO: *<u>Jason</u>, besides the Creightons, <u>want</u> two tickets.*

YES: *<u>Jason</u>, besides the Creightons, <u>wants</u> two tickets.*

NO: *<u>Rachel and Jim</u>, no less than Mary, <u>seems</u> anxious to hear the results of the contest.*

YES: *<u>Rachel and Jim</u>, no less than Mary, <u>seem</u> anxious to hear the results of the contest.*

NO: *The <u>sound</u> of the bells always <u>please</u> me.*

YES: *The <u>sound</u> of the bells always <u>pleases</u> me.*

IN SENTENCES WHERE THE SUBJECT FOLLOWS THE VERB, BE ESPECIALLY CAREFUL TO DETERMINE THE SUBJECT AND MAKE IT AGREE WITH THE VERB.

NO: *In the back of the room <u>sits</u> many of my <u>friends</u>.*

YES: *In the back of the room <u>sit</u> many of my <u>friends</u>.*

NO: *Into the dark <u>stares</u> her black <u>cats</u>.*

YES: *Into the dark <u>stare</u> her black <u>cats</u>.*

NO: *There is many <u>pictures</u> on the wall.*

YES: *There are many pictures on the wall.*

NO: *There lives the Murphys.*
YES: *There live the Murphys.*

NO: *On her side of the river is three parks.*
YES: *On her side of the river are three parks.*

NO: *There remains many things yet to discuss.*
YES: *There remain many things yet to discuss.*

NO: *Far ahead of the others scouts Marion and Sam.*
YES: *Far ahead of the others scout Marion and Sam.*

NO: *There is no other avenues for us to follow.*
YES: *There are no other avenues for us to follow.*

WHEN SINGULAR SUBJECTS ARE JOINED BY EITHER...OR, NEITHER...NOR, OR OR NOR, THE VERB IS SINGULAR.

NO: *Either the principal or the football coach usually attend the dance.*
YES: *Either the principal or the football coach usually attends the dance.*

NO: *I'm sure that neither the lawyer nor the accountant are to blame.*
YES: *I'm sure that neither the lawyer nor the accountant is to blame.*

NO: *The Harrisons or the Jacobs knows the directions.*
YES: *The Harrisons or the Jacobs know the directions.*

NO: *The acorn or the walnut or the pecan fall first to the ground.*
YES: *The acorn or the walnut or the pecan falls first to the ground.*

IF ONE OF THE SUBJECTS IS PLURAL AND ONE SINGULAR, MAKE THE VERB AGREE WITH THE SUBJECT NEAREST IT.

NO: *Neither the cat nor the dogs is eating today.*
YES: *Neither the cat nor the dogs are eating today.*

NO:	*Either the <u>students</u> or the <u>teacher</u> <u>speak</u> at any one time in <u>this</u> classroom.*
YES:	*Either the <u>students</u> or the <u>teacher</u> <u>speaks</u> at any one time in <u>this</u> classroom.*

NO:	*The <u>piano</u> or the <u>violins</u> <u>plays</u> the loudest.*
YES:	*The <u>piano</u> or the <u>violins</u> <u>play</u> the loudest.*

NO:	*Neither <u>Mr. Phillips</u> nor my <u>friends</u> <u>knows</u> the play.*
YES:	*Neither <u>Mr. Phillips</u> nor my <u>friends</u> <u>know</u> the play.*

NO:	*Neither the <u>clouds</u> nor the <u>sun</u> <u>cheer</u> me today.*
YES:	*Neither the <u>clouds</u> nor the <u>sun</u> <u>cheers</u> me today.*

REMEMBER THAT A WORD USED AS A WORD OR AS THE TITLE OF A PARTICULAR WORK, EVEN IF IT IS PLURAL, REQUIRES A SINGULAR VERB.

NO:	*<u>Politics</u> <u>are</u> a noun.*
YES:	*<u>Politics</u> <u>is</u> a noun.*

NO:	*Montaigne's <u>ESSAYS</u> <u>have</u> always <u>been</u> one of my favorite books.*
YES:	*Montaigne's <u>ESSAYS</u> <u>has</u> always <u>been</u> one of my favorite books.*

NO:	*The <u>NEW YORK TIMES</u> <u>print</u> informative, reliable stories on most all subjects.*
YES:	*The <u>NEW YORK TIMES</u> <u>prints</u> informative, reliable stories on most all subjects.*

NO:	*<u>Aerobics</u> <u>remain</u> a best-seller month after month.*
YES:	*<u>Aerobics</u> <u>remains</u> a best-seller month after month.*

4.3 VERBALS

Verbals are words that originate from verbs. They can be confusing because they are like verbs and, at the same time, like other parts of speech. They have <u>verb forms</u>: the *gerund*, *infinitive*, and *participle*. And, like verbs, they can show tense, take complements, and be modified by adverbs. They <u>function</u>, however, like other parts of speech: the *noun*, *adjective*, and *adverb*. In short, verbals are verb forms that do not function as verbs.

4.3.1 THE GERUND

The *gerund* is a verb form that ends in -ing and is used as a *noun*.

> *Writing a paper is not as easy as you might think.*
>
> *John's laughing in class caused the principal to reprimand him.*
>
> *Running requires diligence.*
>
> *Jenny likes walking to work when it is sunny and cool.*

The gerund has two tenses: <u>present</u> and <u>perfect</u>. (The perfect tense refers to action occurring before the action represented by the main verb in the sentence.)

> present: *walking, speaking*
>
> perfect: *having walked, having spoken*

> *While walking home I met my sister.*
>
> *Eating all those cookies gave Johnny a stomach ache.*
>
> *Having completed the job earned me a vacation.*
>
> *Having missed the bus made us late for the concert.*

4.3.2 THE INFINITIVE

The *infinitive* is the basic form of the verb, usually preceded by the preposition "to." It may function as a *noun*, an *adjective*, or an *adverb*.

> *to write*   *to run*
>
> *to laugh*   *to walk*

> *It is not as easy to write a paper as you might think.*
>
> *John started to laugh when the teacher explained the meaning of the word "obscene".*
>
> *To run every day requires diligence.*
>
> *Jenny likes to walk to work when it is sunny and cool.*
>
> *He wouldn't dare laugh in the principal's office.* (omission of "to")

The infinitive also has two tense forms: present and perfect.

present: *to walk, to speak*

perfect: *to have walked, to have spoken*

Mary had to walk to the bus stop.

Harold wasn't supposed to eat the cookies.

We were supposed to have completed the job by Monday.

We were sorry to have missed the concert.

4.3.3 THE PARTICIPLE

The participle is a verb form that usually ends in *-ing* or *-ed*, and less frequently, *-en*, *-d*, or *-t*. It functions primarily as an adjective, although it may also serve as an adverb.

The laughing boy was silenced by harsh words.

Frightened, the little girl hid behind her mother.

Poached eggs are delicious.

The stolen purse was retrieved by the police yesterday.

Grasping the life preservers, the exhausted passengers fell into the dinghy waiting below.

The participle has three tense forms: present, past and perfect.

Present participle: *walking, speaking*

Past participle: *walked, spoken*

Perfect participle: *having walked, having spoken*

The man walking down the street is her uncle.

The people eating in the restaurant are obviously wealthy.

The paper, having been written and revised, was ready for publication.

The table, well constructed, was on display at the museum.

4.4 EXERCISES

A. Fill in the correct form of the verb in the present tense.

    1. She _____ sad to leave. *(to be)*

    2. They _____ to lock the door occasionally.
                              (to forget)

    3. We _____ the dog for a walk each morning.
                              (to take)

B. Fill in the correct tense of the verb in the parentheses.

    1. I _____ fifty pages by tomorrow. *(to read, future)*

    2. We _____ in the concert. *(to sing, past)*

    3. He _____ class on Mondays and Wednesdays.
                              (to teach, present)

    4. You _____ the dress without permission.
                              (to take, past)

    5. It _____ once spring arrives. *(to grow, future)*

    6. The bee _____ her while she was on vacation.
                              (to sting, past)

    7. He _____ many Broadway plays.
                      (to cast, past perfect)

    8. He _____ the plane tomorrow if the skys are clear.
                      (to fly, future progressive)

    9. They _____ furniture all afternoon.
                      (to choose, present perfect progressive)

    10. You _____ your ticket before the train arrived.
                      (to buy, past perfect progressive)

C. In agreement, the verb must agree with the subject in
    both number and person. Therefore, it is important to
    recognize both the subject and verb in a sentence. In
    the following examples, underline the verb once and the
    subject twice.

    1. John, along with the rest of his family, is attending
        the picnic.

4.4 EXERCISES

2. The music on the radio always relaxes me.

3. Every student has a trip planned for the winter recess.

4. Sandy and John, along with Peter, seem very happy to be finalists in the contest.

5. There go the Greens on their trip.

D. In the following sentences make the necessary corrections.

1. Either her mother or her father usually drive her to school on rainy days.

2. There is, if I calculated right, two hundred dollars left in my bank account.

3. Mary, and the rest of her friends, were late for the test.

4. Economics are a major taught in many colleges.

5. The first years of high school is the most difficult.

6. Aristotle's <u>Poetics</u> have always been read widely.

7. The noise from all those fans were distracting.

8. Neither the chorus nor the actors knows their parts.

9. Each of us are going away for the weekend.

10. Neither the grass nor the flowers was growing well.

11. She had wore that dress before.

12. Tomorrow, I find out the information you need.

13. There is no other means to meet tuition costs.

14. We had mistook them to be famous.

15. Tuesday, I goes to my friends' house for dinner.

16. All the members, including John, wants Greta to be re-elected.

17. The boy turned around after she called him.

18. Lay down on the couch and relax.

19. George, along with the Greens, are vacationing in Vermont.

20. She sat the vase on the piano.

21. She sewn that dress during spring vacation.

4.4 EXERCISES

22. Yesterday, Melissa finds the book she had been looking for all week.

23. Before they could get to the movies, the car broke down.

24. She had laid down when the phone rang.

25. Michael's new short story, like all of his stories, are well written.

26. The hum of the insects distract me.

27. We rung the bell several times but no one answered.

28. Last Monday, he picks out the costumes for the production.

29. Next year, we go away for the summer.

30. At the front of the auditorium sits two distinguished professors.

31. The book is laying on the table.

32. Before Aunt Mary arrived, I dressed the baby.

33. Next month, I graduate from high school.

34. If we had knew you were coming we would have prepared a special dinner.

35. Every one of you understand the material.

E. Underline the verbals in the following sentences. Indicate whether the verbal is a gerund, a participle, or an infinitive.

1. Attending the theater is enjoyable; I usually like to go once a year.

2. Having read the book, he began to discuss the implications of the plot on the theme.

3. Having mowed the grass in the back yard, I sat down to have a glass of water.

4. The stolen dog was found on the roadside and returned to its owners.

5. Linda started to giggle when she heard him sing.

6. Grabbing the keys, Mary Jo hurriedly ran to the car parked on the street.

7. I like to wake to music in the morning.

8. Losing her balance, she fell into the lake.

4.4 EXERCISES

9. I have work to do, so I must leave the rehearsal early today.

10. Reading music is relatively simple after a few months of practice.

CHAPTER 5

ADJECTIVES AND ADVERBS

Adjectives and adverbs always appear in relation to some other word; they are modifiers. They have so much in common that they can be considered together.

> Living well is the best revenge.
>
> The shrewd guess, the fertile hypothesis, the courageous leap to a tentative conclusion--these are the most valuable coin of the thinker at work. -- J. Bruner
>
> The opposing team played an aggressive, sophisticated game.

All of the words underlined above are adjectives. You can recognize an adjective because it always refers to a noun, a pronoun, or any other word or group of words playing the part of a noun. Adjectives qualify, describe, or limit nouns or pronouns.

The underlined words in these sentences are all adverbs. Adverbs refer to verbs, adjectives or other adverbs.

> Slowly he turned and saw her waiting patiently there.
>
> She thought deeply about her most dearly loved companion, then left immediately with a little more hope that she could still find him soon.
>
> It is more easily understood if you read quickly through the least difficult chapters first.

As you can see, modifiers are a part of almost all sentences. Although only the subject (noun or pronoun) and the verb are necessary for a complete sentence, such a simple construction is unusual. "Time flies" is an example of such a minimal expression. Even a short sentence such as "The dog barks." contains a modifier. The more complex a sentence becomes, the more modifiers are used. Modifiers help to make the meaning of a sentence more clear and exact. A careful study of them is important to good writing.

5.1 RECOGNIZING ADVERBS AND ADJECTIVES

Sometimes we can recognize a word as an adverb or an adjective by its form, but sometimes the same form of a word is used for both functions. In these cases, it is difficult to distinguish between an adverb and an adjective. One clue is that many adverbs end in "ly". Here is a comparison of some basic nouns, their adjectival and their adverbial forms:

NOUN	ADJECTIVE	ADVERB
truth	*truthful*	*truthfully*
intention	*intentional*	*intentionally*
theory	*theoretical*	*theoretically*
hour	*hourly*	*hourly*
coward	*cowardly*	*cowardly*
shore	*ashore*	*ashore*

Not all adverbs end in "ly," and to complicate matters, there are a number of adjectives which do.

Examples of adverbs that do not end in "ly":

now	*quite*	*still*
then	*when*	*almost*
soon	*down*	*here*
very	*yet*	*too*
often	*around*	

I'll be quite unhappy if you don't say yes.

Now they are ready to be very helpful.

Call me often if you still love me.

Examples of adjectives that end in "ly":

lovely	*orderly*	*timely*
lively	*friendly*	*lonely*
homely	*kindly*	*jolly*
likely		

Mary is a <u>lovely</u> girl, but her sister Jean is <u>homely</u>.

It was a <u>timely</u> decision that led to <u>friendly</u> relations between the two schools.

On the <u>lonely</u> cross-country drive, he wasn't <u>likely</u> to meet many <u>kindly</u> strangers.

Some words have the same form whether they are used as an adjective or an adverb. For example:

well	*deep*	*right*
early	*fast*	*wrong*
little	*late*	*better*
very	*above*	*hard*
much	*long*	

The difference between adverbs and adjectives actually depends not on distinctive endings but on the way the word functions in a sentence. If the word modifies a noun it is an adjective. If it modifies an adjective, adverb or verb, it is an adverb.

Is he <u>well</u>? (adjective)

Does he type <u>well</u>? (adverb)

The teacher was <u>quick</u> to stop the noise. (adjective)
If you want to see a sight, come <u>quick</u>! (adverb)

<u>Fast</u> though he was, he couldn't keep up with Stevens.
  (adjective)
How <u>fast</u> can you run? (adverb)

There are some adverbs that have two acceptable forms--one with an "ly" ending and one without the "ly" ending. Usually, the "ly", or longer form, is preferred--especially for writing. The shortened form is more likely to be used in speaking informally. Examples of these adverbs are:

direct – directly	*slow – slowly*
tight – tightly	*loose – loosely*
high – highly	*loud – loudly*
quick – quickly	*cheap – cheaply*
deep – deeply	*sure – surely*
near – nearly	*close – closely*
considerable – considerably	

Though we often drop the "ly" in speech, it is usually not correct, and should be avoided.

NO: *You look <u>real</u> great tonight.*

YES: *You look <u>really</u> great tonight.*

NO: *Don't talk so <u>loud</u>.*

YES: *Don't talk so <u>loudly</u>.*

NO: *You <u>sure</u> have all the luck.*

YES: *You <u>surely</u> have all the luck.*

5.2 COMPARISON OF ADJECTIVES

Adjectives and adverbs have three forms that show a greater or lesser degree of the characteristic of the basic word: the <u>positive</u>, the <u>comparative</u> and the <u>superlative</u>. The basic word is called the positive. The comparative is used to refer to two persons, things or groups. The superlative is used to refer to more than two people, things or groups; it indicates the greatest or least degree of the quality named. Most adjectives of one syllable become comparative by adding "er" to the ending and become superlative by adding "est" to the ending. In adjectives ending with "y", the "y" changes to "i" before adding the endings.

Examples of comparison of adjectives:

POSITIVE	COMPARATIVE	SUPERLATIVE
little	*littler, less*	*littlest, least*
happy	*happier*	*happiest*
late	*later*	*latest*

brave	*braver*	*bravest*
lovely	*lovelier*	*loveliest*
long	*longer*	*longest*
friendly	*friendlier*	*friendliest*
fast	*faster*	*fastest*
shrewd	*shrewder*	*shrewdest*
tall	*taller*	*tallest*

Adjectives of two or more syllables usually form their comparative degree by adding "more" (or "less") and form their superlative degree by adding "most" (or "least").

Examples of comparison of adjectives of two or more syllables:

POSITIVE	COMPARATIVE	SUPERLATIVE
handsome	*more handsome* *less handsome*	*most handsome* *least handsome*
timid	*more timid* *less timid*	*most timid* *least timid*
tentative	*more tentative* *less tentative*	*most tentative* *least tentative*
valuable	*more valuable* *less valuable*	*most valuable* *least valuable*
endearing	*more endearing* *less endearing*	*most endearing* *least endearing*

Some adjectives are irregular; their comparatives and superlatives are formed by changes in the words themselves.

Examples of comparison of irregular adjectives:

POSITIVE	COMPARATIVE	SUPERLATIVE
good	*better*	*best*
many *much* *some*	*more*	*most*
bad	*worse*	*worst*

little	*less*	*least*
far	*farther*	*farthest*
	further	*furthest*

Def.: *farther*-- referring to a physical distance.
 further-- referring to a differing degree, time or quality.

Adverbs are compared in the same way as adjectives of more than one syllable: by adding "more" (or "less") for the comparative degree and "most" (or "least") for the superlative.

Examples of comparison of adverbs:

POSITIVE	COMPARATIVE	SUPERLATIVE
easily	*more easily* *less easily*	*most easily* *least easily*
quickly	*more quickly* *less quickly*	*most quickly* *least quickly*
truthfully	*more truthfully* *less truthfully*	*most truthfully* *least truthfully*

Some adverbs are irregular; some add "er" or "est".

Examples of comparison of irregular adverbs:

POSITIVE	COMPARATIVE	SUPERLATIVE
little	*less*	*least*
well	*better*	*best*
far	*farther*	*farthest*
badly	*worse*	*worst*
fast	*faster*	*fastest*
soon	*sooner*	*soonest*
much	*more*	*most*
hard	*harder*	*hardest*
close	*closer*	*closest*

The comparative and superlative indicate not only the differences in the degree of the quality named, but also in the number of things discussed.

Use the comparative to compare two things:

Mary is the more lazy of the two.

I've tasted creamier cheese than this.

James is the shorter of the two boys.

Of the two, I like Gail better.

My teacher is kinder than yours.

This book is more interesting than that one.

Use the superlative to compare more than two things:

Mary is the laziest girl I know.

This is the creamiest cheese I've ever tasted.

James is the shortest boy in the class.

Of those five people, I liked Gail best.

My teacher is the kindest in the school.

This book is the most interesting of the three.

There are some words to which comparison does not apply, since they already indicate the highest degree of a quality. Here are some examples:

Adverbs and adjectives with no comparison:

immediately	*superlative*	*first*
last	*very*	*unique*
uniquely	*universally*	*perfect*
perfectly	*exact*	*complete*
correct	*dead*	*deadly*
preferable	*round*	*perpendicularly*
square	*third*	*supreme*
totally	*infinitely*	*immortal*

5.2.1 ERRORS TO AVOID IN COMPARISON

Do not combine two superlatives:

> *NO:*   *That was the <u>most bravest</u> thing he ever did.*
>
> *YES:* *That was the <u>bravest</u> thing he ever did.*
>
> *NO:*   *He grew up to be the <u>most handsomest</u> boy in the town.*
>
> *YES:* *He grew up to be the <u>most handsome</u> boy in the town.*

Do not combine two comparatives:

> *NO:*   *Mary was <u>more friendlier</u> than Susan.*
>
> *YES:* *Mary was <u>friendlier</u> than Susan.*
>
> *NO:*   *The puppy was <u>more timider</u> last week.*
>
> *YES:* *The puppy was <u>more timid</u> last week.*

5.3 COMPARISON WITH "OTHER" OR "ELSE" OR "OF ALL"

A common mistake when comparing members of a group is to forget to indicate that the item being held up for comparison is still a part of the rest of the group to which it is being compared. The addition of "other" or "else" to the comparative makes this relationship more clear. If the superlative is used, adding "of all" makes the meaning more definite and emphatic.

> *NO:* *She is a better piano player than any pianist in our group.* (Is she part of the group?)
>
> *YES:* *She is a better piano player than any <u>other</u> pianist in our group.* (It is now clear that she is a member of the group.)
>
> *NO:* *Our dog is smarter than any on the block.* (Does the dog live on the block?)
>
> *YES:* *Our dog is smarter than any <u>other</u> on the block.* (Now it is obvious that the dog lives on the block.)
>
> *NO:* *Your car is the fastest car in the neighborhood.*

(Whose neighborhood?)

YES: Your car is the fastest of all the cars in the neigh-borhood. (Your car belongs in the neighborhood.)

5.4 CONFUSION WITH ADVERBS AND ADJECTIVES

5.4.1 LINKING VERBS

There are two categories of verbs after which an adjective form is used instead of an adverb form. When using these verbs, it is easy to make a mistake and use an adverb instead of an adjective since, logically, the modifier seems to refer to the verb, but actually it refers to the subject.

Use an adjective after:

1. Forms of the verb "to be" and other nonaction verbs such as:

seem	*appear*	*become*
remain	*prove*	

The boy was studious. (studious boy)

She appears happy. (happy girl)

The prediction proved incorrect. (incorrect prediction)

Jim remained depressed. (depressed Jim)

2. Verbs of the senses such as:

taste	*feel*	*look*
smell	*sound*	

Marianne feels sick. (sick Marianne)

That apple tastes good. (good apple)

Those girls look beautiful. (beautiful girls)

The music sounded crisp and clear. (crisp and clear music)

The cake smelled appetizing. (appetizing cake)

NO: *Those girls look beautifully.* *(WRONG)*

Those girls are beautifully. *(illogical)*

YES: *She appears happy.*

She is happy. *(logical)*

NO: *I feel badly.* *(WRONG)*

I am badly. *(illogical)*

YES: *The rose smells sweet.*

The rose is sweet. *(logical)*

YES: *The music sounded crisp and clear.*

The music is crisp and clear. *(logical)*

Sometimes the modifier refers to the verb, describing or clarifying the manner of the action. In this case, the adverbial form must be used.

She felt cautiously for the lightswitch. *(cautiously felt)*

The music sounded loudly in her ears. *(loudly sounded)*

Her parents appeared immediately after she called. *(immediately appeared)*

5.5 THE ARTICLES--LIMITING ADJECTIVES

The most commonly used adjectives are the shortest--the articles *a, an,* and *the* that signal nouns. *A* and *an* are called indefinite articles because they refer to any unspecified member of a group or class. *The* is called a definite article because it refers to a specific member of a group or class. They function as adjectives because they limit a noun or pronoun.

Indefinite articles--*a* and *an*		Definite article--*the*
a pen	*a refrigerator*	*the pen* (a specific pen)
a tree	*a secretary*	*the tree* (a specific tree)
an onion	*an error*	*the error* (a specific error)

A is used before words beginning with a consonant sound,

and *an* before words with a vowel sound. This is an important distinction; it is not the spelling that determines whether to use *a* or *an*, but the sound.

an umbrella	*BUT*	*a university*
a radio	*BUT*	*an R.C.A. record*
an hour	*BUT*	*a human being*

5.5.1 ERRORS TO AVOID IN USING THE ARTICLE

Do not use *the* before "both":

NO: *Let's see the both of them on Saturday.*
YES: *Let's see both of them on Saturday.*

NO: *He helped the both of them out of the car.*
YES: *He helped both of them out of the car.*

Do not use *a* or *an* after phrases ending with "of", such as "kind of","sort of","type of","manner of":

NO: *What kind of a car did he buy?*
YES: *What kind of car did he buy?*

NO: *He was not that sort of a person.*
YES: *He was not that sort of person.*

The following possessive forms of pronouns, *my*, *our*, *your*, *her*, *his*, *its*, *their* are also limiting adjectives. They help to define or limit the noun or the pronoun. Indefinite, demonstrative, interrogative and relative pronouns also function as adjectives when they modify a noun or pronoun.

Take this road.

Will you hand me some silverware.

Whose sweater is this?

That was my paper which won.

The girl whose purse was stolen was very upset.

5.6 COMPOUND ADJECTIVES PRECEDING AND FOLLOWING A NOUN

Just as there are compound nouns, there are compound adjectives. When two or more words are used together as a single adjective to modify a noun, they are joined by <u>hyphens:</u>

> That was a <u>thirst-quenching</u> drink.
>
> He is a <u>well-known</u> man.
>
> When he entered the room he saw a <u>half-asleep</u> child.
>
> John's was an <u>all-inclusive</u> study of birds.
>
> They wanted a <u>one-inch</u> margin.

If the adjectives follow the noun, however, they are <u>generally</u> not hyphenated:

> He wanted a drink that was <u>thirst quenching</u>.
>
> That man is <u>well known</u>.
>
> They wanted a margin of <u>one inch</u>.
>
> When he entered the room, he saw the child <u>half-asleep</u>.*
>
> John's study was <u>all-inclusive</u>. *

*The spelling of compounds is constantly changing. Notice that "all-inclusive" and "half-asleep" are hyphenated whether they precede or follow the noun. It is best to consult a dictionary to be certain about hyphenating compounds. (see "THE HYPHEN").

Also, use a hyphen with the prefixes "ex-", "self-" and "all-":

> The ex-President is still involved in world affairs.
>
> He died of a self-inflicted wound.

Finally, a hyphen is used between any prefix of a proper noun or adjective.

> The weather is pleasant in mid-May.
>
> Americans enjoyed the prosperity of post-WWII.

5.7 EXERCISES

AJECTIVES AND ADVERBS

A. In the following sentences identify and label the adjectives and adverbs.

1. That was an interesting answer to a difficult question.
2. He answered the question honestly.
3. They swim in deep water.
4. Which dress did you buy?
5. The musicians perform often.
6. Don't tie the package so tightly.
7. She almost passed the test.
8. It is obvious he made the right choice.
9. Are they late?
10. That is a likely excuse.
11. Though he was right, he had a difficult time defending his point.
12. How early can you arrive?
13. There were several members missing at the meeting.
14. Her grandfather is a jolly old man.
15. Does he work hard?

B. COMPARATIVE AND SUPERLATIVE: In the following sentences make the changes indicated in the parentheses. Also indicate if the comparative or superlative form is an adverb or an adjective.

1. He was sad to leave. (superlative)
2. She ran as fast as the others on the team. (comparative)
3. Throughout school, they were good in math. (superlative)
4. This class is as interesting as the European history class. (superlative)
5. He arrived as soon as I did. (comparative)
6. The test was as hard as we expected. (superlative)
7. He responded to the interviewer as candidly as Tom. (comparative)

5.7 EXERCISES

   8. The beggar had less possessions than she. (superlative)

   9. That answer is perfectly correct. (superlative)

  10. She read the part best. (comparative)

C. In the following sentences, make the necessary corrections.

1. He is the tallest boy in the school.
2. She is a better fielder than any player on our team.
3. Your grass is the greenest on the block.
4. That park is larger than any park in the state.
5. The test was the hardest one given this year.

D. In the following sentences, complete the example with the correct form of the word given in the parentheses.

1. The solution seems _____. (clear)
2. They looked _____ (diligent) for the lost money.
3. The evidence proved her _____. (innocent)
4. Joe looks _____. (sick)
5. The police appeared _____ (quick) after the alarm sounded.

E. Correctly complete the following sentences with the appropriate article.

1. Please read me _____ fifth name on the list.
2. What type of _____ dog did they choose?
3. That was _____ honest mistake.
4. Can you donate _____ dollar to the charity?
5. It is apparent there is _____ increase in the rent.

F. Correctly complete the following sentences using the words given in the parentheses.

1. That was a _____ paper (well/written)
2. The job he did was _____ (first/rate)
3. School will begin in _____. (mid/September)
4. That is a _____ play. (little/known)
5. He is now the _____. (ex/champion)

CHAPTER 6

PREPOSITIONS

"Some people write by day, others by night. Some people need silence, others turn on the radio. Some write by hand, some by typewriter, some by talking into a tape recorder. Some people write their first draft in one long burst and then revise; others can't write the second paragraph until they have fiddled endlessly with the first." --On Writing Well
-William Zinsser

Between New York and Chicago, we came upon two strange signs that kept us inside the car despite our strong desire to go outside around daybreak. For hours, we stayed on the road contrary to our plan, with those signs reappearing before our eyes long after they had disappeared from our sight.

All the underlined words in the preceding paragraphs are prepositions. Prepositions are connecting words; they connect the word or words that follow them (called the object of the preposition) with some other part of the sentence. They illustrate a relationship between words. The preposition and the word or group of words that follows it is called the prepositional phrase, which can function in a sentence as an adjective, adverb or noun.

There are two kinds of prepositions--simple, one-word prepositions and group prepositions.

6.1 SIMPLE PREPOSITIONS

at the office	*by the seashore*	*for your love*
down south	*on the desk*	*like her sister*
through the door	*about the house*	*within three weeks*
beside the bed	*over the top*	*behind his chair*

| *except* you | *across* town | *with* kind greet-ings |

6.2 GROUP PREPOSITIONS

according to	*in conjunction with*	*in place of*
because of	*as well as*	*in addition to*
by means of	*in front of*	*in spite of*

There are only a few rules governing the use of prepositions. Learning to use the correct preposition is really a matter of developing a good sense of what sounds right. This is acquired by listening and by trying to write the way we talk. Of course, some aspects of speech must be formalized for writing.

6.2.1 ERRORS TO AVOID

In speech, there is a tendency to either overuse or omit necessary prepositions. This should be eliminated in formal writing.

Examples of Overuse:

> NO: *She just couldn't start <u>in</u> to do her homework.*
>
> YES: *She just couldn't start to do her homework.*
>
> NO: *Let's divide <u>up</u> the orange.*
>
> YES: *Let's divide the orange.*
>
> NO: *When did they finally get <u>down</u> to the problem?*
>
> YES: *When did they finally get to the problem?*

Examples of Omission:

> NO: *She was concerned <u>about</u> Jamie and his many dogs.*
>
> YES: *She was concerned <u>about</u> Jamie and <u>about</u> his many dogs.*
>
> NO: *Mr. Liles gained his reputation <u>by</u> hard work and honest dealings with his customers.*
>
> YES: *Mr. Liles gained his reputation <u>by</u> hard work and <u>by</u> honest dealings with his customers.*

NO: _At_ her office and home, she tried to be the same person.

YES: _At_ her office and _at_ home, she tried to be the same person.

Need for different prepositions in the same phrase

NO: Mother was both influenced and annoyed _with_ her doctor.

YES: Mother was both influenced _by_ and annoyed _with_ her doctor.

NO: The Joneses were familiar and fond _of_ Rembrandt paintings.

YES: The Joneses were familiar _with_ and fond _of_ Rembrandt paintings.

NO: We have become reconciled and accepting _of_ our fate.

YES: We have become reconciled _to_ and accepting _of_ our fate.

Overconcern with placement:

Although in the past it was considered incorrect English to end a sentence with a preposition, it is no longer so. Current usage (everyday speech) and rhythm often necessitate putting a preposition at the end of a sentence. Excessive attention paid to following this outdated rule can result in some unnatural and confusing sentences:

NO: Tell me for what you are looking.

YES: Tell me what you are looking _for_.

NO: She had no one to whom to turn.

YES: She had no one to turn _to_.

NO: They had many problems about which to talk.

YES: They had many problems to talk _about_.

6.3 IDIOMATIC PREPOSITIONS

Idioms are expressions that are characteristic of a particular language. The idiomatic use of prepositions has become quite popular in the English language. Here, prepositions are used after certain verbs, participles, nouns and adjectives. New forms and meanings of these idiomatic prepositions are continually coming into the language. It is advisable to consult the dictionary to determine whether an expression is idiomatic, for example, "similar to", or unidiomatic such as "similar with". Other usage labels such as informal, vulgar, or slang should also be checked so the writer can determine whether the expression is appropriate for that particular piece of writing. The following is a partial listing of some standard idiomatic prepositions. For further discussion of idioms, see "USING THE DICTIONARY."

abstain from

acquit of

addicted to

adept in

adhere to

agree to (a thing)

agree with (a person)

angry at (a thing)

angry with (a person)

averse to

capable of

characteristic of

compare to (for an example)

compare with (to illus-
        trate a point)

concern in

concerned with

desire for

desirous of

devoid of

differ about

differ from (things)

differ with (a person)

different from

disagree with

envious of

expert in

foreign to

hint at

identical with

independent of

infer from

inseparable from

jealous of

oblivious of

prerequisite to

prior to

proficient in

profit by

prohibit from

protest against

reason with

regret for

repugnant to

sensitive to

separate from

substitute for

superior to

sympathize with

tamper with

disdain for   *unmindful of*
distaste for
empty of

6.4 EXERCISES

A. <u>PREPOSITIONS</u> -- In the following sentences underline the prepositional phrase.

1. They went into the house to get their coats.

2. According to the report, crime has gone down.

3. They wouldn't think of going without you.

4. He sat in front of us at the theatre.

5. She was heading toward the lake when I saw her.

B. In the following sentences make the necessary additions and deletions.

1. Let's finish up the assignment.

2. He was interested and fascinated with physics.

3. She had learned of his life and his times through reading.

4. They were both repelled and driven toward the space creature.

5. Tell me on what he left it.

6. Let's go over to James' house tomorrow.

7. She always had an interest and an aptitude for science.

8. It took a long time to get at the problem.

9. She looked like her sister and her mother.

10. Her belief and dedication to the cause were total.

C. <u>IDIOMATIC PREPOSITIONS</u> -- Complete the following sentences with the standard preposition.

1. He couldn't agree _____ Margaret's interpretation.

2. She had nothing but disdain _____ John and his friends.

3. They hoped to profit _____ the scheme.

4. Physics I is a prerequisite _____ that class.

5. It is impossible to reason _____ her.

CHAPTER 7

CONJUNCTIONS

Not only Susan but both Andrew and Samuel were either for fighting or for getting out immediately since no help had arrived. Although they all wanted to stay, the fighting was bound to begin again, and this time with more force than before.

The underlined words in the preceding paragraph are all conjunctions. Like prepositions, conjunctions are connecting words. They connect words, phrases or clauses. There are four kinds of conjunctions: coordinating, conjunctive adverbs, correlative and subordinating.

7.1 COORDINATING CONJUNCTIONS

Coordinating conjunctions connect parts of a sentence that are equivalent. It is fairly simple to determine whether sentence parts are equivalent: words are equal to other words; phrases are equal to phrases; main clauses are equal to main clauses; and minor (or subordinating) clauses are equal to minor clauses. The following are commonly used coordinating conjunctions:

and	*but*	*yet*
for	*or*	*nor*
both	*moreover*	*whereas*

They may join a word to another word:

Mom and Dad	*Jill or Susan*	*firm yet kind*
run and jump	*sink or swim*	*slowly but surely*

--a phrase to another phrase:

out of sight and out of mind

of great insight <u>but</u> of poor judgment

hurrying down the street <u>or</u> meandering through the woods

--a minor (subordinate) clause to another minor clause:

She insisted that she knew him <u>yet</u> (that she) had not told him the story.

John could not remember where he mailed the letter <u>or</u> when he left the office.

-- a main clause to another main clause:

I wanted to attend the meeting, <u>whereas</u> John never had the slightest intention of going.

Jean worked hard, <u>for</u> she knew she would not keep her job if she did not.

The old grammar rule "Never start a sentence with "and" or "but" is no longer adhered to. Sometimes using a coordinating conjunction to start a sentence is very effective.

She said she would leave early. <u>And</u> she did.

They all expected him to win. <u>But</u> he lost.

7.1.1 ERRORS TO AVOID

When using a coordinating conjunction, be sure that the sentence elements you are joining are equivalent.

> *NO: Her main interests were <u>that she succeed</u> and <u>skiing</u>.*
>
> *YES: Her main interests were <u>success</u> and <u>skiing</u>.*
> OR
> *YES: Her main interests were <u>that she succeed</u> and <u>that she ski regularly</u>.*

> *NO: She loved him dearly but <u>not his dog</u>.*
>
> *YES: <u>She loved him dearly</u> but <u>she did not love his dog</u>.*

> *NO: Jason left his sister <u>out in the cold</u> and <u>alone</u>.*
>
> *YES: Jason left his sister <u>out in the cold</u> and <u>by herself</u>.*
> OR
> *YES: Jason left his sister <u>outside</u> and <u>alone</u>.*

7.2 CONJUNCTIVE ADVERBS

Conjunctive adverbs have a dual role. They connect independent clauses and also illustrate the relationship between the two clauses. Although the clause introduced by the conjunctive adverb is grammatically sufficient, a logical relationship exists with the other clause. Since the conjunctive adverb basically introduces a modifying clause, it is less of a connector than the coordinating conjunction.

Clauses joined by conjunctive adverbs must be separated by either a period or a semicolon. The following are some conjunctive adverbs and transitional phrases, which serve the same function.

therefore	*furthermore*	*nevertheless*
however	*besides*	*indeed*
consequently	*moreover*	*thus*
accordingly	*still*	*hence*
for this reason	*likewise*	*on the contrary*
for example	*in addition*	*in the first place*
on the other hand	*at the same time*	

He won the competition in Moscow; consequently he went on to have an outstanding career as a soloist.

Jackie had been sick for many months; thus she needed more time to complete the assignment.

He had shown a great deal of potential; and for this reason, he was given the job.

I would like to see the play; however, I have no time.

His essay provided many fine insights. Moreover, it was well written.

7.3 CORRELATIVE CONJUNCTIONS (USED IN PAIRS)

These conjunctions are always used in pairs which illustrate clearly that the parts they connect in a sentence are equivalent (parallel). The correlative conjunctions are:

both--and   *not only--but also*

either--or   neither--nor

if--then   since--therefore

The parts they join must be similar in form:

Either the secretary or the treasurer must preside.

Since you were late therefore I cannot seat you.

Neither your crying nor your protesting will change my opinion.

7.3.1 ERRORS TO AVOID

When using correlative conjunctions, a common mistake that is made is to forget that each member of the pair must be followed by the same kind of construction.

NO: Her reaction not only was strong but also immediate.

YES: Her reaction not only was strong but was also immediate.

OR

YES: Her reaction was not only strong but also immediate.

NO: They complimented them both for their bravery and they thanked them for their kindness.

YES: They both complimented them for their bravery and thanked them for their kindness.

NO: She came neither to help the cause nor hinder it.

YES: She came neither to help the cause nor to hinder it.

NO: Either give me your promise you'll stay three years or your letter of resignation.

YES: Either give me your promise you'll stay three years or turn in your letter of resignation.

OR

YES: Give me either your promise you'll stay three years or your letter of resignation.

NO: Her job was both to teach the course and its design.

YES: Her job was both to teach the course and to design it.

OR

YES: Her job was both to teach and to design the course.

OR

YES: *Her job was both <u>the teaching of the course</u> and <u>its design.</u>*

7.4 SUBORDINATING CONJUNCTIONS

Not all sentences are composed solely of equal parts. Usually there are parts that are essential to the main idea and others that serve as support or give additional information about the main idea. Subordinate conjunctions are used to help connect parts of a sentence that are unequal. Some subordinate conjunctions are:

as	*because*	*as though*
since	*although*	*though*
provided	*after*	*before*
in order that	*when*	*while*
until	*if*	*unless*
how	*so that*	*that*
where		

Typically, these words introduce descriptive (subordinate) clauses and connect them to the main clauses. For example:

I'll go with you <u>provided</u> that you drive.

<u>Because</u> she ran quickly, she arrived on time.

He will call the office <u>after</u> his meeting.

She won't come <u>unless</u> you invite her.

<u>If</u> you want less noise, move to the country.

Faulty coordination can also be corrected by placing ideas of lesser importance in a subordinate position.

NO: *He did not practice driving <u>and</u> he failed his road test.*

YES: *<u>Because</u> he did not practice driving, he failed <u>his road</u> test.*

NO: *The election returns came in Tuesday night <u>and</u> weren't published in the morning paper.*

YES: *<u>Although</u> the election returns came in Tuesday*

night *they weren't published in the morning*
paper.

NO: *Wordsworth published "Tintern Abbey" <u>and</u> gained much recognition.*

YES: *<u>After</u> Wordsworth published "Tintern Abbey" he gained much recognition.*

7.5 OTHER ERRORS TO AVOID

<u>Improper use of *while*</u>

<u>While</u> refers to time and should not be used as a substitute for <u>although</u>, <u>and</u> or <u>but</u>.

NO: *<u>While</u> I'm usually interested in Fellini movies, I'd rather not go tonight.*

YES: *<u>Although</u> I'm usually interested in Fellini movies, I'd rather not go tonight.*

NO: *He wrote the script <u>while</u> I assembled the slides.* (unless the meaning is "at the same time")

YES: *He wrote the script <u>and</u> I assembled the slides.*

<u>Improper use of *where*</u>

<u>Where</u> refers to a place or location. Be careful not to use it when it does not have this meaning.

NO: *We read in the paper <u>where</u> they are making great strides in DNA research.*

YES: *We read in the paper <u>that</u> they are making great strides in DNA research.*

NO: *A good time is <u>where</u> time goes by quickly.*

YES: *A good time is <u>when</u> time goes by quickly.*

7.6 EXERCISES

A. Identify the conjunctions used in the following sentences. Label coordinating conjunctions (COOR), conjunctive adverbs (CONJ), correlative conjunctions (CORR) and subordinating conjunctions (SUB).

1. They couldn't decide whether to go to the beach or to go to the movies.

2. I don't dislike John. On the contrary, he's one of my best friends.

3. Both Linda and her sister were at the concert.

4. He smiled as though he had won the contest.

5. I wanted to read the book but I couldn't find a copy of it in the library.

6. She didn't study for the test; nevertheless, she earned one of the highest grades.

7. Either you make a decision or you forget the offer.

8. Until you came there was no one to help with the dishes.

9. I know you studied geometry last year; still I would like to review some of the basic concepts.

10. Mary not only won the race but she also set a record.

11. I have finished the assignment; whereas John has just begun.

12. Since you studied algebra you can therefore take calculus.

13. Mother would like you to do the wash while she is gone. In addition, she wants you to clean the the basement.

14. He will begin the work provided that you give him a down-payment.

15. Before we leave let's call Aunt Joan.

16. If you apologize then I will help you with your home-work.

17. Judith read the novel; however, she did not enjoy it.

18. We were all on time. But she was late.

19. He wasn't satisfied although he had checked his an-swers twice.

7.6 EXERCISES

B. Make the necessary corrections in the following sentences.

1. John's best assets are his personality and swimming.

2. I heard on the radio where the play is closing this week.

3. I was reading the paper and the phone rang.

4. Susan ate vegetables often but not fruits.

5. Please send me an answer to the question or opinions on the project.

6. While I'm tired from the trip, I'll attend the concert tonight.

7. Mary's goal is to study hard and pass the test.

8. He produced the play while she directed it.

9. A good essay is where the ideas are clearly articulated.

10. The class wanted neither to read the book nor do the assignment.

C. Correct the faulty coordination in the following sentences. Also make sure that the conjunction expresses the exact relationship between the two ideas.

1. We were lost and you found the map.

2. Ellen had lost the race and still maintained her confidence.

3. The book was priceless and it was a first edition.

4. She had heard the lecture Monday night and was very confused.

5. The president was a charismatic leader and he had many followers.

6. The crop was poor and the price of corn went up.

7. He mowed the lawn and she sipped iced tea.

8. I'll go to the movie and you drive.

9. The picnic was cancelled and it rained.

10. You do the dishes and I'll clean the dining room.

CHAPTER 8

PARTS OF THE SENTENCE

8.1 SUBJECT & PREDICATE

A sentence is a group of words that makes sense, ending with a period, exclamation point, or question mark. It is the basic unit of communication. Every sentence, unless it is a command, has a subject and a predicate.

SUBJECT	PREDICATE
Harry	*drives his father's truck.*
We	*saw a flock of geese.*
Benjamin Franklin	*was a printer.*
Elephants	*never forget.*
San Francisco	*is full of hills.*

The subject is the topic of the sentence. It announces what the sentence is about. The predicate is what is said about the subject. The subject is generally a noun or pronoun, as in the examples above. Sometimes gerunds, infinitives, phrases and clauses can also act as the subject. When they do, they are called nominals (a word that acts like a noun).

> *His singing woke the whole house.*
>
> *What we don't know is his age.*
>
> *To fly has always been man's dream.*

A simple subject is a noun or pronoun without any modifiers.

> *Joe walks his dog in the morning.*
>
> *The door shut with a bang.*

118

We read aloud in the evenings.

The movie was really too long.

The birds were singing in the garden.

The train rumbled past.

Everyone knows his name.

In the evening the crickets begin to chirp.

Commands have no apparent subject. Due to the nature of the command, it is tacitly understood to be <u>you</u>.

Run as fast as you can!

Add up these numbers and tell me the answer.

Jeff, please buy me a newspaper.
(Jeff is the person addressed, not the subject.)

<u>Compound subjects</u> are two or more simple subjects connected by <u>and</u> or <u>or</u>.

Music and dancing followed dinner.

Check or money order must accompany each application.

The <u>complete subject</u> is the simple subject and all its modifiers.

The blue house at the end of the block is now for sale.

The women who sang at the party left on the 5:00 train.

Two rather round fellows, Tweedledum and Tweedledee, stood side by side looking at her.

A few Cadillacs were parked outside the building.

The predicate always contains a verb. The <u>simple predicate</u> is the verb without any modifiers.

Gail laughed.

The gorillas bellowed.

Edgar Allan Poe wrote some rather grim stories.

Did you hear about the party?

Bring your copy of the book.

Theresa dried her hair.

Is everybody here?

A <u>compound predicate</u> is two simple predicates connected by <u>and</u> or <u>or</u>.

> *The audience <u>shouted and clapped</u> when the curtain fell.*
>
> *You either <u>saw</u> the film <u>or heard</u> about it.*

8.2 TRANSITIVE VERBS AND OBJECTS

Verbs can express action. The subject is the one who does the action. The noun that receives the action is the <u>object</u>.

> *Harold studied <u>physics</u>.*
>
> *Alice put <u>her hand</u> through the mirror.*
>
> *Who built <u>the Sphinx</u>?*
>
> *Charles invited <u>Mary and David</u>.*
>
> *This machine cleans <u>carpets</u>.*
>
> *Can you drive this <u>car</u>?*
>
> *When did Alan paint his <u>boat</u>?*
>
> *Dennis is fixing the <u>telephone</u>.*
>
> *Tie your <u>shoes</u>!*

When a verb takes an object to complete its meaning, it is called a <u>transitive verb</u>. A transitive verb usually needs an object to make sense.

> *NO: The company built.*
>
> *YES: The company built an alarm into the system.*
>
> *NO: The team brings.*
>
> *YES: The team brings its own equipment.*
>
> *NO: Ellen and Harry thanked.*
>
> *YES: Ellen and Harry thanked their lucky stars.*
>
> *NO: We all make.*
>
> *YES: We all make our own breakfast.*

Sometimes a transitive verb can do without an object, as in: *<u>Harold studied</u>,* or *<u>This machine cleans</u>.* However, they usually take an object.

A noun or pronoun is called the <u>direct object</u> when it is the direct receiver of the action of the verb, as in the examples above. The <u>indirect object</u> is the noun or pronoun that tells us to <u>who</u> or <u>for whom</u> the action was done. In the following examples, the underlined words are indirect objects.

Did they leave <u>us</u> any cake?   (Did they leave any cake for <u>us</u>?)

Call <u>me</u> a cab.   (Call a cab for <u>me</u>.)

Michael wrote a song for <u>Daphne</u>.

Did you give the key to <u>Jennifer</u>?

Are you talking to <u>me</u>?

Alan bought <u>Susan</u> a racing bike. (Alan bought a racing bike for <u>Susan</u>.)

Toss <u>him</u> the catalog.   (Toss the catalog to <u>him</u>.)

I do not think that they will sing to <u>me</u>.

8.3 INTRANSITIVE VERBS AND COMPLEMENTS

<u>Intransitive verbs</u> are verbs that do not take an object. They can stand alone with the subject.

> *The sun also <u>rises</u>.*
>
> *A baby must <u>crawl</u> before he can <u>walk</u>.*
>
> *What made Dennis <u>laugh</u>?*
>
> *Maryann <u>blushed</u>.*
>
> *Did Nero <u>fiddle</u> while Rome <u>burned</u>?*
>
> *<u>Think</u> before you <u>speak</u>.*
>
> *Ellen <u>danced</u>.*

Intransitive verbs often use complements to complete their meaning. Complements are quite different from objects. They do not receive the action of the verb, but complete its meaning.

> *The sun rises <u>early</u>.*
>
> *The baby can crawl <u>quite quickly</u>.*
>
> *What made Dennis laugh <u>so loudly</u>?*
>
> *Maryann blushed <u>when Charles teased her</u>.*

The cut bled <u>profusely</u>.

The shooting stars fell <u>like rain</u>.

Mr. Pickwick coughed <u>nervously</u>.

Notice that all the complements in the above examples are adverbs or adverbials (a word or group of words that acts like an adverb). Intransitive verbs use adverbs as complements. Copulative verbs can use adjectives as complements, but intransitive verbs cannot.

NO: The baby can crawl so <u>quick</u>!

YES: The baby can crawl so <u>quickly</u>!

NO: He moved <u>cautious</u>.

YES: He moved <u>cautiously</u>.

NO: Anthony's car rides <u>smooth</u>.

YES: Anthony's car rides <u>smoothly</u>.

NO: Walk <u>slow</u>!

YES: Walk <u>slowly</u>!

NO: The band was playing <u>bad</u>.

YES: The band was playing <u>badly</u>.

NO: The river froze <u>quick</u>.

YES: The river froze <u>quickly</u>.

8.4 COPULATIVE VERBS AND COMPLEMENTS--SENSING VERBS

A verb describes either an action or a state of being. Transitive and intransitive verbs describe actions. <u>Copulative verbs</u> only describe states of being. The verb <u>to be</u> is the most common copulative verb. Others are: *act, appear, seem, become, remain, look, sound, feel, smell, taste, grow.*

The complement of a copulative verb refers to the subject. It modifies or completes the meaning of the subject.

The complement of a copulative verb is either a noun:

Ben Johnson was a <u>contemporary</u> of Shakespeare.

Moby Dick is a complex <u>book</u>.

Oedipus became <u>king</u>.

He did not seem like a good <u>mechanic</u>.

a nominal (a word or group of words that acts like a noun):

His argument was <u>that man is a rational creature</u>.

Jim's aim is <u>to write the great American novel</u>.

or an adjective:

His head feels <u>cool</u>.

After he heard the news, Lawrence looked quite <u>pale</u>.

The mist smelt <u>foul</u>, like rotten eggs.

Your squash will taste <u>better</u> with some butter.

If I look <u>good</u>, it's because I feel <u>good</u>!

Copulative verbs always take an adjective for a complement rather than an adverb. This may sometimes sound funny, but it makes better sense.

<u>COMPARE</u>

<u>Sensing Verb</u>	<u>Intransitive Verb</u>
The radiator felt cool.	*Ralph behaved coolly.*
Some fruits are quite bitter.	*A spoiled child was crying bitterly.*
Watermelon tastes sweet.	*Birds are piping sweetly.*
Try to act humble.	*The old man spoke humbly.*

8.5 SENTENCE ORDER

Usually the parts of the sentence appear in this order:

SUBJECT-VERB-DIRECT OBJECT

| *James* | *smokes* | *cigars.* |
| *Bill* | *collects* | *lizards.* |

If there is an indirect object, it appears in front of the direct object

SUBJECT-VERB-INDIRECT OBJECT-DIRECT OBJECT

Harry   *saved*   *me*   *some chicken*.

unless it follows *to* or *for*

$$SUBJECT\text{-}VERB\text{-}DIRECT\ OBJECT <\genfrac{}{}{0pt}{}{to}{for}> INDIRECT\ OBJECT$$

I   *told*   *the story*   *to*   *Margie*.

If the verb is transitive or copulative, the order is

SUBJECT - VERB - COMPLEMENT

Marie   *laughs*   *excessively*.
George   *is*   *a good businessman*.

Of course, sentences do not always appear in this order. Commands, for example, have no subject:

VERB - OBJECT

Drive   *the car*.
Milk   *the cow*.

The order of parts may be altered in a question. The example below gives the question in SUBJECT-VERB-DIRECT OBJECT order, then shows a few alternatives.

Plato wrote <u>*The Republic*</u>?

Did Plato write <u>*The Republic*</u>?

(SUBJECT-VERB-OBJECT)

Was <u>*The Republic*</u> *written by Plato?*

(SUBJECT-VERB-COMPLEMENT)

The use of expletives will also change word order. *It* and *there*, when used as introductory words, are <u>expletives</u>. They fill the space of the subject, but an expletive is never the actual subject of a sentence.

There are bears in the woods nearby.

(VERB-SUBJECT-COMPLEMENT)

It is good for brothers to live in peace.

(VERB-COMPLEMENT-SUBJECT)

Word order is also changed for emphasis:

I have no objections. (Normal order)

Objections have I none. (Emphasis on the object, "ob-jections")

We cleaned the house quickly. (Normal order)

The house we cleaned quickly. (Emphasis on "house")

Birds and airplanes were in the sky. (Normal order)

In the sky were birds and airplanes. (Emphasis on the phrase "in the sky")

I will follow you even to death. (Normal order)

Even to death will I follow you. (Emphasis on the phrase "even to death")

We crept to the window quietly, like thieves. (Normal order)

Quietly, like thieves, to the window we crept. (Emphasis on how we were creeping)

These changes in word order, especially the last type of change--for emphasis--add variety and color to writing.

8.6 PHRASES

All this time the Guard was looking at her, first through a telescope, then through a microscope, and then through an opera-glass. At last he said, "You're travelling the wrong way," and shut up the window and went away.

"So young a child," said the gentleman sitting opposite to her (he was dressed in white paper), "ought to know which way she's going, even if she doesn't know her own name!"

A Goat, that was sitting next to the gentleman in white, shut his eyes and said in a loud voice, "She ought

to know her way *to the ticket-office*, even if she doesn't
know her alphabet!"

Lewis Carroll, *Through the Looking Glass*

All the underlined groups of words are phrases. <u>Phrases</u> fill
in many of the details that make a sentence interesting. For
example, the sentence *"We sat."* could turn into any of the
following by the addition of phrases:

We sat for hours, looking at the painting.

On the cliffs by the sea we sat, watching the sunset.

We sat by Amelia at the restaurant.

A <u>phrase</u> is a group of connected words without a subject or
predicate. A <u>prepositional phrase</u> begins with a preposition,
and contains a noun and its modifiers. Some examples are:

Take me to the opera.

I think Mark is in his room.

What is in the box that came from Hawaii?

George works best under pressure.

After the movie, let's drive by the river.

The noun in a prepositional phrase is called the <u>object of the
preposition.</u>

A prepositional phrase can be used as an adjective:

The woman on the phone is Jane.

The mysteries of outer space are waiting for us.

*Henry felt like the Sword of Damocles was hanging over
his head.*

an adverb:

Anthony was caught between the horns of a dilemma.

A large rabbit dove under the ground.

Carol lifted the weight with apparent ease.

Without doubt, the council decided for the best.

or a noun:

In the evening is as good a time as any.

A gerund phrase contains a gerund and its modifiers. It is always used as a noun.

Reading blueprints is not as easy as it sounds.

Thoreau placed great value on living simply.

Wandering in and out of stores is Harriet's favorite way of passing time.

Living well is the best revenge.

Leaving at night helped us avoid the traffic. (gerund phrase as subject)

They accused him of robbing the bank. (gerund phrase as the object of the preposition *of*)

Having missed the bus, we arrived at the party late. (participial phrase as modifier)

Exercising regularly is seizing an opportunity to keep healthy. (gerund phrase as subject and as predicate nominative)

An infinitive phrase contains an infinitive and its modifiers. It can also be used as a noun, adjective, or adverb.

To know him is to know his brother. (Noun)

A waiter's job is to serve a table. (Noun)

It's important to have good language to suit the occasion. (Adjective)

Tom brought a book to lend me. (Adjective)

We'll have to run to catch the train. (Adverb)

No one had time to complete the extra-credit problem. (infinitive phrase used as an adjective modifying the noun *time)*

We managed to arrive on time. (infinitive phrase as an adverb, modifying the verb *manage)*

We hope to win the race. (infinitive phrase as object of verb)

* The present infinitive also expresses the future time. We hope now to win the race in the future.

A participial phrase contains a participle and its modifiers. It is used as an adjective to modify a noun or a pronoun.

The gentleman standing in the aisle is the owner.

Having said his piece, he sat down.

The fisherman, weathered by experience, calmly took the line.

Walking the balance beam, she was extremely careful.
(The participial phrase modifies *she*. *Balance beam* is the direct object of the participle *walking*.)

Missing the bus by a second, we decided to take a taxi.
(The participial phrase modifies *we*. *Bus* is the object of the participle *missing*.)

Running into the house, Mary tripped on the rug.
(*Running into the house* is the participial phrase. But the prepositional phrase *into the house* is also a part. It modifies the participle *running*. The participial phrase modifies *Mary*. *House* is the object of the preposition *into*.)

The incorrect use of the participial phrase results in a stylistic error called the dangling modifier. For further information on these phrases, see the section "DANGLING MODIFIERS."

8.7 CLAUSES

A clause differs from a phrase in that it has a subject and a predicate.

> *PHRASE: We're planning a trip to the museum.*
>
> *CLAUSE: We're planning a trip so we can see the museum.*
>
> *PHRASE: After a swim, we'll have lunch.*
>
> *CLAUSE: After we swim, we'll have lunch.*
>
> *PHRASE: Bill told them during dinner.*
>
> *CLAUSE: Bill told them while they were eating dinner.*
>
> *PHRASE: In the box he found some old letters.*
>
> *CLAUSE: When he looked in the box he found some old letters.*
>
> *PHRASE: Harriet laughed at the comedian.*
>
> *CLAUSE: Harriet laughed whenever the comedian opened his mouth.*

Often a relative pronoun like *that, which, who, whom,* or *whoever* will act as the subject of a clause.

> *Tell me who was singing.*
>
> *Everyone who signed the sheet is eligible.*
>
> *Arnold knew something that was generally unknown.*
>
> *Do you remember which kind is better?*
>
> *Give it to whomever has the most need.*

In introductory clauses, the use of *that* and *which* often presents a problem for the writer. The difference is simple: If the clause is essential to the meaning of the sentence, use *that.* If the clause is not essential to the meaning of the sentence, use *which* and set off the clause with commas.

> *THAT:* *The book that contained the formula was missing.* (It is essential that the formula is in the missing book.)
>
> *WHICH:* *The book, which contained the formula, was missing.* (It is only essential that the book is missing.)
>
> *THAT:* *We saw a movie that lasted two hours.* (The length of the film is important.)
>
> *WHICH:* *We saw a movie, which lasted two hours.* (The length of the film is less important.)
>
> *THAT:* *The car that Al was driving got a flat tire.*
>
> (Out of several cars, Al's car was the one to get a flat tire.)
>
> *WHICH:* *The car, which Al was driving, got a flat tire.* (This car got a flat tire and, incidentally, Al was driving.
>
> *THAT:* *The titles that are underlined will be printed in italics.* (Only the underlined titles will be printed in italics. The rest of the titles will not.)
>
> *WHICH:* *The titles, which are underlined, will be printed in italics.* (All of the titles are underlined, and they will all be printed in italics.)
>
> *THAT:* *Alan owns a boat that sailed around the world.* (Alan's boat sailed around the world.)
>
> *WHICH:* *Alan owns a boat, which sailed around the world.* (The fact that it sailed around the world is incidental.)

THAT:	Paul brought a wine that is ten years old. (This wine is ten years old.)
WHICH:	Paul brought a wine, which is ten years old. (Paul brought some wine.)
THAT:	Let me show you the dress that I bought today. (I bought this dress today and I want to show it to you.)
WHICH:	Let me show you this dress, which I bought today. (I'll show you the dress. I bought it today.)

8.8 SENTENCE ERRORS

STRUCTURAL PROBLEMS

8.8.1 DANGLING PARTICIPLES

The dangling participle is the most bizarre and comical of all sentence errors. Because it is such a glaring error, it stops the reader dead in his tracks. The sentence lacks clarity, and the reader must take a moment to determine the meaning.

NO:	I saw a fish sitting on a bench by the brook.
YES:	I saw a fish while I was sitting on a bench by the brook.
NO:	I saw two stores and a movie theater walking down the street.
YES:	Walking down the street, I saw two stores and a movie theater.
NO:	Harold watched the painter gaping in astonishment.
YES:	Harold watched the painter and gaped in astonishment.
NO:	You can see the moon standing in the front yard.
YES:	If you stand in the front yard, you can see the moon.
NO:	Sheila hung the towels dripping wet.

YES: Sheila hung the dripping wet towels.

NO: He found a nest of tiny birds mowing the lawn.

YES: He found a nest of tiny birds while mowing the lawn.

NO: Andy saw the ferry boat pulling into his parking space.

YES: Andy was pulling into his parking space when he saw the ferry boat.

NO: No one noticed the danger, playing so enthusiastically.

YES: No one noticed the danger. They were playing so enthusiastically.

8.8.2 MISPLACED MODIFIERS

There are other types of modifiers that cause confusion when they are out of place. It is not important to learn the names of the various errors one could make, but it is important to avoid these errors. In general, structure a sentence logically by placing the modifier near the word it modifies. In each of the following examples, a phrase is out of place.

NO: By digging around the roots, the tree can be removed without damage.

YES: By digging around the roots, you can remove the tree without damage.

NO: On correcting the test, his errors became apparent.

YES: His errors became apparent when the test was corrected.

NO: After showing the experiment, it was time to go home.

YES: After he showed us the experiment, we had to go home.

NO: The door was shut while dancing with Debbie.

YES: The door was shut while I was dancing with Debbie.

NO: Before baking cookies, the hands must be washed.

YES: Before baking cookies, be sure to wash your hands.

The difficulty with the sentences above is that the reader is not sure who is doing what. *"The door was shut while dancing with Debbie,"* is ambiguous. <u>Who</u> is dancing with Debbie? The door? It is important to be clear about the sense of every sentence. The meaning can completely change when a word or phrase is moved to the proper place.

NO: *My mother gave chocolate to her friends with soft centers.*

YES: *My mother gave chocolates with soft centers to her friends.*

NO: *Newspapers reported his travels in every country.*

YES: *Newspapers in every country reported his travels.*

NO: *The champagne was served to guests in paper cups.*

YES: *The champagne was served in paper cups to the guests.*

NO: *I said today that I would help him.*

YES: *I said that I would help him today.*

NO: *Jane said on her way upstairs that she would straighten the picture.*

YES: *Jane said that she would straighten the picture on her way upstairs.*

NO: *I saw two boys throwing rocks through my window.*

YES: *Through my window I saw two boys throwing rocks.*

NO: *Henry put his candy in a drawer that he ate later.*

YES: *Henry put his candy in a drawer so he could eat it later.*

NO: *This powder can cure a cold with a funny smell.*

YES: *This funny-smelling powder can cure a cold.*

NO: *I know a man with a wooden leg named Smith.*

YES: *I know a man named Smith who has a wooden leg.*

NO: *He climbed the ladder with a bad leg.*

YES: *He climbed the ladder even though he had a bad leg.*

There are some words that must appear immediately before the word they modify or they will cause confusion. These are words like _almost, only, just, even, hardly, nearly not,_ and _merely_.

NO: _Jane almost polished the plate until it shined._

YES: _Jane polished the plate until it almost shined._

NO: _Harry only was affected by the news._

YES: _Only Harry was affected by the news._

NO: _The store on the corner only sells that toaster._

YES: _Only the store on the corner sells that toaster._

NO: _Everybody can't fit in my car._

YES: _Not everybody can fit in my car._

NO: _Steve nearly made $50 last night._

YES: _Steve made nearly $50 last night._

NO: _Dan almost took the whole cake._

YES: _Dan took almost the whole cake._

NO: _Charles merely smiled to look friendly._

YES: _Charles smiled merely to look friendly._

NO: _Andy just asked a question to annoy the speaker._

YES: _Andy asked a question just to annoy the speaker._

Look at how the meaning can change when the modifier is moved around in the following series of sentences.

Only life exists on earth.   (There is nothing else on earth except life.)

Life only exists on earth.   (Life does nothing but exist on earth. This sentence is somewhat ambiguous.)

Life exists only on earth.   (Nowhere else but on earth can one find life.)

Life exists on earth only.   (More emphatic than the last sentence, but says the same thing.)

Place _only_ and other modifiers close to the word that they modify. This is the best way to avoid ambiguity.

8.8.3 AMBIGUOUS PRONOUNS

Can you make sense out of the following paragraph?

> *Harry called to David while he was coming down the stairs.*
> *David told Harry that he should not talk for long since*
> *he had laryngitis. Harry said that it wouldn't take long.*
> *Then he told David that he had seen him raking leaves.*
> *He said that he made a big mistake. David asked what*
> *he had done wrong. Harry replied that everyone could*
> *see where he made his mistake that looked closely.*

Try it now:

> *Harry was coming down stairs when he called out to David.*
> *David said, "I can't talk very long; I have laryngitis."*
> *Harry replied, "This won't take long. I saw you when*
> *I was raking leaves, and I want to tell you that you made*
> *a big mistake." David asked, "What did I do wrong?"*
> *Harry replied, "Anyone who looked closely could see what*
> *you did wrong."*

Pronouns can add grace and variety to our writing. Yet they
become a problem when we use these too much, or when it is
difficult to tell exactly what the pronoun is referring to. This
is the most important lesson to learn about pronouns: make
sure that it is clear what the pronoun is referring to.

> NO: *It was dark and it was heavy, and I tripped over*
> *it and dropped it down the stairs.*

> YES: *It was dark, and the box was heavy. I tripped*
> *over something and dropped the box down the stairs.*

> NO: *When Mary saw Anne, she told her that she was*
> *going to help her with the project.*

> YES: *When Mary saw Anne, Anne told her that she would*
> *be happy to help Mary with the project.*

> NO: *Whenever it rains, it always makes that funny noise.*

> YES: *Whenever it rains, the furnace always makes that*
> *funny noise.*

> NO: *He was late but he didn't know it.*

> YES: *He was late but Andy didn't know it.*

> NO: *She couldn't say anything; she had forgotten her*
> *name.*

> YES: *She couldn't say anything; she had forgotten the*

woman's name.

NO: *I laughed when I saw the bird standing on his head.*

YES: *I laughed when I saw the bird standing on Lloyd's head.*

NO: *Benjamin went to the doctor and found out that he was very sick.*

YES: *Benjamin went to the doctor, and found out that the doctor was very sick.*

<u>Who</u> and <u>which</u> and <u>that</u> can create similar problems. Make sure that it is clear what each pronoun refers to .

NO: *Tom said he saw a cute little monkey who usually doesn't care about animals.*

YES: *Tom, who usually doesn't care about animals, said he saw a cute little monkey.*

NO: *He charged too high a price for the job that is generally considered unethical.*

YES: *He charged so high a price that it is generally considered unethical.*

NO: *I saw an organ grinder and a monkey who had a handlebar moustache.*

YES: *I saw an organ grinder and his monkey, and the man had a handlebar moustache.*

NO: *My father is quite famous as a chemist, which I know nothing about.*

YES: *My father is quite famous as a chemist, but I know nothing about chemistry.*

NO: *The machine took the cup that detected a defect.*

YES: *The machine detected a defect, so it took the cup away.*

When a reader sees a pronoun, he looks for a nearby noun to determine what the pronoun stands for. If the noun is too far away, the reader has to hunt for it. This slows down and irritates the reader.

NO: *I shut the door and concentrated only on my work. It was old and heavy and shut out every sound.*

YES: *I had to concentrate on my work, so I shut my*

135

door. *It's old and heavy, and it keeps out every sound.*

NO: *I took my car on the freeway to try out the engine. It's long and flat, and you can go pretty fast.*

YES: *I wanted to try out the engine, so I took my car on the freeway. It's long and flat, and you can go pretty fast.*

8.8.4 LACK OF PARALLEL STRUCTURE

When ideas are similar, they should be expressed in similar forms. When elements of a sentence are similar, they too should appear in similar form.

NO: *She likes sun, the sand, and the sea.*

YES: *She likes the sun, the sand, and the sea.*

NO: *The instructor explained the problem, method, and the tools that we were to use.*

YES: *The instructor explained the problem, method, and tools that we were to use.*

NO: *George is always singing, drumming, or he will play the guitar.*

YES: *George is always singing, drumming, or playing the guitar.*

NO: *Charlene's car skidded, turned sideways, then comes to a stop.*

YES: *Charlene's car skidded, turned sideways, and came to a stop.*

NO: *The janitor stopped, listened a moment, then he locked the door.*

YES: *The janitor stopped, listened a moment, then locked the door.*

NO: *Why did you make Carl feel useless and as if he was unimportant?*

YES: *Why did you make Carl feel useless and unimportant?*

NO: *It was a time when people were more aware and they were outspoken.*

> YES: *It was a time when people were more aware and outspoken.*

Whenever _and_ or _or_ are used in a sentence, they must connect equal parts. Words are paired with words, phrases with phrases, clauses with clauses, and sentences with sentences. All these pairs must be parallel; they must have the same form.

> NO: *Washington was said to be "First in war, first for peace, and first in the hearts of his countrymen."*

> YES: *Washington was said to be "First in war, first in peace, and first in the hearts of his countrymen."*

> NO: *Her family went to London, to Amsterdam, and they even saw Rome and Paris!*

> YES: *Her family went to London, to Amsterdam, and even to Rome and Paris!*

> NO: *You can use this form to apply or if you want to change your status.*

> YES: *You can use this form to apply or to change your status.*

> NO: *Is it our thoughts or what we do that matters more?*

> YES: *Is it what we think or what we do that matters more?*

> NO: *Debby noticed the way Margie talked and how she kept looking at the desk.*

> YES: *Debby noticed how Margie talked, and how she kept looking at the desk.*

Pairs of connectives (like _both/and, either/or, neither/nor, not only/but also_) usually connect parallel structures.

> NO: *That book was both helpful and contained a lot of information.*

> YES: *That book was both helpful and informative.*

> NO: *So, my father said, "Either you come with us now, or stay here alone."*

> YES: *So, my father said, "Either you come with us now, or you stay here alone."*

> NO: *Here we either turn left or right, but I forget which.*

YES: *Here we turn either left or right, but I forget which.*

NO: *Karen bought the table both for beauty and utility.*

YES   *Karen bought the table for both beauty and utility.*

NO: *Jim was influenced both by his brother and his friends.*

YES   *Jim was influenced by both his brother and his friends.*

NO: *Janet's coat is at either the restaurant or my car.*

YES: *Janet's coat is either at the restaurant or in my car.*

8.8.5 SENTENCE FRAGMENTS

"Where did you go?"

"To the new movie theater. The one on Valley Street."

"Where on Valley Street?"

"Just past the train station, and across the street from the Post Office."

"See a good movie?"

"The best. Really funny, but serious, too."

"Sounds good."

Probably neither of the people in the conversation above realized that they were not using complete sentences. Only the first question, *"Where did you go?"* is a complete sentence. The rest are sentence fragments.

A sentence fragment is only a part of a sentence since it is usually missing a subject or a verb.

NO: *So illogical!*
YES: *It is so illogical!*

NO: *To try again? To fail again?*
YES: *Could he try again? Would he fail again?*

NO: *And danced for joy at the news.*
YES: *Then she danced for joy at the news.*

NO: *A tree as old as your father.*

YES: *The tree is as old as your father.*

NO: *No time for long speeches.*

YES: *This is no time for long speeches.*

NO: *Only for love, you see.*

YES: *They did it only for love, you see.*

NO: *No one. Not even the teacher.*

YES: *No one, not even the teacher, could do it.*

NO: *A place very near to my heart.*

YES: *It will always remain a place very near to my heart.*

In conversation, there is a tendency to speak in sentence fragments (as in the one above), and so they often appear in our writing. Proofreading and revision, however, can help to correct this error.

There are two ways to correct a sentence fragment. The first is to supply whatever is missing, as was done above. The other way is to attach the fragment to the sentence before or after it.

NO: *When I jog, especially in the early morning. I sometimes see the morning star.*

YES: *When I jog, especially in the early morning, I sometimes see the morning star.*

NO: *Because he was wrong. That's why he was embarrassed.*

YES: *He was embarrassed because he was wrong.*

NO: *Ted has made that mistake, too. But only when he wasn't paying attention.*

YES: *Ted has made that mistake, too, but only when he wasn't paying attention.*

NO: *Tom stood there, biting his nails. Nervously thinking about his debts.*

YES: *Tom stood there biting his nails nervously, thinking about his debts.*

NO: *Think of a book that everyone has heard of. Like* <u>*Tom Sawyer*</u>*.*

YES: *Think of a book that everyone has heard of, like*

Tom Sawyer.

NO: _Is this the only solution? To fight like animals?_

YES: _Is this the only solution: to fight like animals?_

_OR_

Is this the onlv solution? Shall we always fight like animals?

NO: _Always and everywhere. She thought of him always and everywhere._

YES: _Always and everywhere, she thought of him._

It is not always incorrect to use sentence fragments. They are used to reproduce conversation, and are also quite effective as questions and exclamations. Some examples are:

How absurd!

Now for some examples.

After all this? Not on your life!

A feeling, nothing more.

Penny wise and pound foolish.

Only by ending this kind of tyranny.

Anyone hurt?

Although properly used sentence fragments can add spark, it is generally best to avoid using them except when more liveliness is needed.

8.8.6 RUN-ON SENTENCES

A run-on sentence is a sentence with too much in it. It usually contains two complete sentences separated by a comma, or two complete sentences totally fused.

NO: _You ate too fast your stomach will hurt._

YES: _You ate too fast and your stomach will hurt._

_OR_

You ate too fast; your stomach will hurt.

NO: _It was a pleasant drive the sun was shinning._

YES: _It was a pleasant drive because the sun was shining._

NO: *They are all similar materials they may not look or feel alike.*

YES: *They are all similar materials although they may not look or feel alike.*

NO: *Susan said we passed the restaurant I think it's further ahead.*

YES: *Susan said we passed the restaurant. I think it's further ahead.*

NO: *Today was so nice tomorrow must be the same.*

YES: *Today was so nice that tomorrow will probably be the same.*

NO: *Everyone knows the answer no one is willing to say.*

YES: *Everyone knows the answer, but no one is willing to say.*

The run-on sentence is a very common error. Sometimes a writer will try to correct it by inserting a comma between the clauses, but this creates another error, a <u>comma splice</u>. The following examples illustrate various ways to correct the comma splice.

NO: *Talk softly, someone is listening.*

YES *Talk softly; someone is listening.*

OR

Talk softly, because someone is listening.

NO: *Laura keeps failing, she keeps trying.*

YES: *Laura keeps failing, but she keeps trying.*

NO: *The train banged and rattled, it was at least sixty years old.*

YES: *The train banged and rattled. It was at least sixty years old.*

NO: *If you know, you must tell us, we will do it.*

YES: *If you know, you must tell us. Then we will do it.*

NO: *Take a hint from me, drive more slowly on this curve.*

YES: *Take a hint from me: drive more slowly on this curve.*

NO: *We were lost, the captain could not see the land.*

YES: *We were lost. The captain could not see the land.*

NO: *The whole family was happy, even old Uncle George was happy.*

YES: *The whole family was happy, even old Uncle George.*

8.9 ERRORS IN STYLE

8.9.1 SHORT, CHOPPY SENTENCES
--SENTENCE VARIATION

Try to read the following passage:

> *There was a table set out under a tree. It was in front of the house. The March Hare and the Hatter were having tea at it. A Dormouse was sitting between them. He was fast asleep. The other two were using it as a cushion. The rested their elbows on it. They talked over its head. "Very uncomfortable for the Dormouse," thought Alice; "only, as it's asleep, I suppose it doesn't mind."*

Notice how quickly you read when the sentences are short; you hardly have enough time to form a picture of the scene. It is as if the writer added each thought as it occurred to him, and in fact, this is usually the case. It is a sure sign of poor writing. Now read the same excerpt the way that Lewis Carroll wrote it.

> *There was a table set out under a tree in front of the house, and the March Hare and the Hatter were having tea at it: a Dormouse was sitting between them, fast asleep, and the other two were using it as a cushion, resting their elbows on it, and talking over its head. "Very uncomfortable for the Dormouse," thought Alice; "only, as it's asleep, I suppose it doesn't mind."*

Sentence variation creates well-balanced, smooth writing which flows and gives the reader the feeling that the writer knows his subject. Although there is nothing grammatically wrong with short sentences, they often separate ideas which should be brought together.

142

NO: *People change. Places change. Alan felt this. He had been away for ten years.*

YES: *On returning after a ten-year absence, Alan had a strong feeling of how people and places change.*

NO: *She looked at the sky. Then she looked at the sea. They were too big. She threw a rock in the ocean. She started to cry. Then she went home.*

YES: *The sky and the sea looked too big. She threw a rock into the ocean, and as it disappeared she began to cry. Then she turned to go home.*

NO: *I have a brother. He is older than I. Everybody thinks I look older. We fight a lot. He doesn't like it. Everybody thinks I look older than him.*

YES: *I have a brother. He is older than I, but everybody thinks that I look older. He doesn't like that, so we fight a lot.*

NO: *I like to sing. I used to sing in a band. The band broke up. Now I don't sing very much.*

YES: *I like to sing. I used to sing in a band, but the band broke up, and now I don't sing very much.*

NO: *I'm happy. The sun is shining. You said it was going to rain. Now we can paint the boat.*

YES: *Didn't you say it was going to rain? Look, the sun is shining; now we can paint the boat.*

NO: *Moby Dick is a book. It is a long book. It is about a whale. A man named Ahab tries to kill it. Herman Melville wrote it.*

YES: *Herman Melville wrote a long book called Moby Dick. It is the story of a struggle of a man against a whale.*

NO: *Did you hear the wind? It was loud. It was whistling at the corners of the house. I heard it last night. I was awake all night.*

YES: *Did you hear the wind last night? I heard it whistling at the corners of the house. It was so loud that it kept me awake all night.*

As a rule, avoid using chains of short, choppy sentences. Organize your thoughts and try to vary the length of your sentences.

8.9.2 WORDINESS

Effective writing means concise writing. <u>Wordiness</u>, on the other hand, decreases the clarity of expression by cluttering sentences with unnecessary words. Of course, all short sentences are not better than long ones simply because they are brief. As long as a word serves a function, it should remain in the sentence. However, repetition of words, sounds, and phrases should be used only for emphasis or other stylistic reasons. Editing your writing will reduce its bulk. Notice the difference in impact between the first and second sentences in the following pairs.

NO: *The medical exam that he gave me was entirely complete.*

YES: *The medical exam he gave me was complete.*

NO: *Larry asked his friend John, who was a good, old friend, if he would join him and go along with him to see the foreign film made in Japan.*

YES: *Larry asked his good, old friend John if he would join him in seeing the Japanese film.*

NO: *I was absolutely, totally happy with the present that my parents gave to me at 7 a.m. on the morning of my birthday.*

YES: *I was totally happy with the present my parents gave me on the morning of my birthday.*

NO: *It seems perfectly clear to me that although he went and got permission from the professor, he still should not have played that awful, terrible joke on the Dean.*

YES: *It seems clear to me that although he got permission from the professor, he still should not have played that terrible joke on the Dean.*

NO: *He went to England by means of a long boat.*

YES: *He went to England by boat.*

NO: *It will be our aim to insure proper health care for each and every one of the the people in the United States.*

YES: *Our aim will be to insure proper health care for all Americans.*

8.9.3 RAMBLING SENTENCES

A rambling sentence continues on and on, and never seems to end.

NO: *The mountain was steep but the road was clear; the sun was shining and we all had the spirit of adventure in our hearts and a song of the open road on our lips, so we took the turn that took our car up that steep mountain road.*

YES: *The mountain was steep, but the road was clear. The sun was shining. All of us had the spirit of adventure in our hearts and a song of the open road on our lips. So, we took our car up that steep mountain road.*

NO: *Everyone knows a person like that, a person who has no concern for others, who will pretend to be a friend, but only because he profits from the relationship, and he never really gives of himself, he just takes, and one cannot call him a friend in any sense of the word.*

YES: *Everyone knows a person like that, a person who has no concern for others. He will pretend to be a friend, but only because he profits from the relationship. He never really gives of himself, he just takes, and one cannot call him a friend in any sense of the word.*

There is often nothing grammatically wrong with a rambling sentence; it is just too long and it interferes with the reader's comprehension. Unfortunately, a writer who makes this kind of error tends to do it a lot. A good rule to follow is this: If a sentence runs for more than two typewritten lines, think twice about it. It should probably be recast.

8.10 EXERCISES

A. In the following sentences, identify the subject by underlining it once, and the predicate by underlining it twice. Also note whether the underlined subject is a complete subject.

1. Susan cultivated the garden.
2. Fix the leak immediately!
3. The man in the brown suit is an undercover cop.
4. Mary, please stop singing!
5. Time and practice helped her win.
6. They laughed and cried when they won the lottery.
7. Only a few people knew the answer to that question.
8. Do your homework!
9. They all laughed loudly.
10. My two friends standing over there are graduating next year.

B. In the following sentences, label the transitive verb (TV), the direct object (DO), the indirect object (IO), the intransitive verb (IV), and the complement (C).

1. The school board added a new wing to the building.
2. Scott wrote a letter to Mary.
3. Who made John study so long?
4. The man must fill out an application before he can take the test.
5. They ran.
6. She drives the car slowly.
7. We were happy when we heard the results.
8. Did you read her the article?
9. She worked diligently.
10. Mow the lawn quickly.

C. In the following sentences, label the copulative verb (CV), the intransitive verb (IV), and the complement (C).

8.10 EXERCISES

1. The economy remained stable.
2. The old man spoke wisely.
3. The plants appear healthy.
4. Children were laughing loudly.
5. Oranges usually taste sweet.

D. Note the order of the following sentences using the verb, subject, direct object, indirect object, and complement.

1. He drives the car cautiously.
2. John called me to apologize.
3. The dog barks loudly.
4. Read the book.
5. They gave the money to Joe.

6. Was <u>King Lear</u> written by Shakespeare?
7. It is important for children to drink milk.
8. There is a gas station in the next town.
9. Did June play the lead?
10. The job we did well.
11. Save your money!
12. The professor gave us the assignment.
13. F. Scott Fitzgerald wrote <u>The Great Gatsby</u>?
14. I gave the book to her mother.
15. He always acts irrationally.

E. In the following sentences, label the <u>prepositional phrase</u> (PR), the <u>infinitive phrase</u> (I), the <u>participle phrase</u> (P) and the <u>gerund phrase</u> (G). In the prepositional phrases, identify the <u>object of the preposition</u> (OP).

1. Reading the book she fell asleep.
2. The police set out to solve the crime and to maintain justice.
3. The woman on the billboard over there is a famous athlete.
4. The man, having painted the house, took a rest.

8.10 EXERCISES

5. Staying in shape is not as difficult as it appears.

6. James solved the problem with pure logic.

7. She found the time to help me with the job.

8. Having completed the mission, he filed a report.

9. The cake in the refrigerator should be saved for tomorrow.

10. Thinking about the future, she opened a savings account.

F. Identify the kinds of phrases in each of the following. Also note what role the phrase plays in relation to the rest of the sentence.

1. Having parked the car we went into the theater.

2. Mary's screaming upset the entire family.

3. She hopes to have made a good impression on the interviewers.

4. Jogging is good exercise.

5. Tom wouldn't dare speak in her presence.

6. While I was reading the newspaper, the phone rang.

7. Mrs. Jones likes singing in the morning.

8. Gaining confidence, she sent them a letter.

9. Greta wanted to open the package.

10. Having forgotten my sweater at the movies, I returned there the next day.

G. In the following sentences, determine whether the underlined portion is a phrase or a clause.

1. The girl in the red dress is my sister.

2. They left the house early so they could get a good seat in the theater.

3. John moved the dresser next to the door.

4. Everyone who attended the meeting is a member.

5. We all knew that was the truth.

8.10 EXERCISES--PART II

A. <u>DANGLING PARTICIPLES/MISPLACED MODIFIERS</u> -- In the following sentences, make the necessary corrections.

1. I saw a stray dog riding the bus this afternoon.
2. The clothing was given to the poor in large packages.
3. I found five dollars eating lunch in the park.
4. We saw two girls riding bicycles from our car.
5. Reading my book quietly, I jumped up when the car crashed.
6. He ran the mile with a sprained ankle.
7. The history majors only were affected by the new requirements.
8. Running quickly to catch the bus, Susan's packages fell out of her arms onto the ground.
9. He just asked the man directions to make sure.
10. He discovered a new route driving home.

B. <u>AMBIGUOUS PRONOUNS</u> -- Through revision, clarify the following sentences.

1. When the car hit the wall, it was badly dented.
2. Since the school picnic was planned for the same day as the test, it had to be changed.
3. John asked the professor and he discovered he was wrong.
4. Mark told Joe he would come if he finished in time.
5. Before the car could go on the road, it had to be repaired.
6. When the police stopped James and Dan on the highway, he asked him for his license.
7. My mother is a well-known artist, which I know little about.
8. June bought a goldfish who usually doesn't like pets.
9. Susan told Kate that her schedule would be more demanding next year.
10. Many people here left the country, to live in the city which is understandable.

C. <u>THAT/WHICH</u> -- Correctly rewrite the following sentences that contain *that* and *which*.

8.10 EXERCISES

Example: Jane owns a car that is a collector's item.

Jane's car is a collector's item.

1. Let me give you the money which I owe you.
2. Show me that lovely painting again.
3. We took a trip which lasted two weeks.
4. The statue that is priceless was stolen.
5. The solution, which solved the problem, was finally discovered.

D. PARALLEL STRUCTURE -- In the following sentences, make the necessary corrections.

1. In the summer I usually like swimming and to waterski.
2. The professor explained the cause, effect, and the results.
3. Mary read the book, studied the examples, and takes the test.
4. Mark watched the way John started the car, and how he left the curb.
5. They bought the house for location and affordability.
6. The movie was interesting and had a lot of excitement.
7. Shakespeare both wrote beautiful sonnets and complex plays.
8. The painting is done either in watercolors or with oils.
9. The lecturer spoke with seriousness and in a concerned tone.
10. Either we forget those plans, or accept their proposal.

E. Determine whether each of the following is a sentence fragment or a run-on sentence and make the necessary corrections.

1. After the rain stopped.
2. Mow the lawn, it is much too long.
3. The settlement you reached it seems fair.
4. When I read, especially at night. My eyes get tired.
5. It was impossible to get through on the phone, the lines

8.10 EXERCISES

were down because of the storm.

6. Is this the only problem? The leaky pipe?

7. Everyone saw the crime, no one is willing to come forth.

8. The weather was bad, she played in the rain.

9. Ellen paced the floor. Worrying about her economics final.

10. Their season was over, the team had lost the play-offs.

F. SHORT SENTENCES/WORDINESS -- Through revision, improve the following sentences.

1. He graduated college. In no time he found a job. Soon after he rented an apartment . He was very happy.

2. The book that she lent me was lengthy. It was boring. I wouldn't recommend it to anyone. There was nothing about the book that I enjoyed.

3. It was raining. We expected to go on a picnic. Now our plans are ruined. We have nothing to do.

4. Whenever anyone telephoned her to ask her for help with their homework she always obliged right away.

5. She liked to paint. She was quite good. Materials are expensive. She can't afford them.

6. Jane is just one of those people who you can't really describe with words.

7. It was time to leave. They hoped they packed everything. There was no time to think. The taxi was outside. It was waiting.

8. The candidate promised he would do what was necessary to lengthen prison terms. This was his major issue. He hoped he was elected.

9. Long Days Journey Into Night is a play. It is a dramatic play. Eugene O'Neill wrote it. The play is also autobiographical.

10. He could have still asked her for her approval.

G. RAMBLING SENTENCES -- Improve the following sentences.

a. The plane was ready to take off; having never travelled by plane before he suddenly felt nervous as the sky ominously turned from grey to black, and threatening bolts of lightning shot across the sky, and thunder echoed in the distance.

8.10 EXERCISES

b. They arrived at the theater early so they could get a front row seat; even though this was the fifth time they saw the film, and practically knew every line by heart, they still screamed at the frightening parts and cried during the sad ending, and left the theater promising to return again for one more showing.

CHAPTER 9

FIGURATIVE LANGUAGE

9.1 FIGURES OF SPEECH

Figurative language helps to create imaginative and detailed writing. A figure of speech is used in the imaginative rather than the literal sense. It helps the reader to make connections between the writer's thoughts and the external world. The following are some commonly used figures of speech.

Simile: A simile is an explicit comparison between two things. The comparison is made by using *like* and *as*.

> *Her hair was like straw.*

> *The blanket was as white as snow.*

Metaphor: Like the simile, the metaphor likens two things. However, *like* or *as* are not used in the comparison.

> *"All the world's a stage."*   *Shakespeare*

> *Grass is nature's blanket.*

A common error is the mixed metaphor. This occurs when a writer uses two inconsistent metaphors in a single expression.

> *The blanket of snow clutched the earth with icy fingers.*

Hyperbole: A hyperbole is a deliberate overstatement or exaggeration used to express an idea.

> *I have told you a thousand times not to play with matches.*

Personification: Personification is the attribution of human qualities to an object, animal, or idea.

The wind laughed at their attempts to catch the flying papers.

9.2 MOOD

The form or the <u>mood</u> of a verb indicates something about the action. In the English language, there are three moods: the indicative, the imperative, and the subjunctive.

<u>The Indicative Mood</u>: When posing a question or making a statement, the indicative mood is used.

> *We are leaving.*   *Are we leaving?*
>
> *It is raining.*   *Is it raining?*

<u>The Imperative Mood</u>: The imperative mood expresses a command, a request, or a direction.

> *Don't touch the sculpture.*
>
> *Take the subway downtown.*
>
> *Read the sign, please.*

<u>The Subjunctive Mood</u>:

a. The subjunctive mood is used in *that* clauses which express motion, resolution, recommendation, command, and hope.

> *I hope that the package will arrive on time.*
>
> *I recommend that the plans be carried through.*
>
> *We requested that an application be sent to your home.*
>
> *Many demanded a refund on the sale item.*

b. The subjunctive mood is also used in *if* clauses which express doubt or the impossibility of the condition.

> *If I had the time, I would join the tennis club.*
>
> *If it was raining, we would go to the movies.*

c. Lastly, the subjunctive mood is used in main clauses to express hope, wish, or prayer.

God save the queen.

May God be with you.

The verb *to be* often gives writers difficulty. In the subjunctive mood, use the verb *to be* as follows:

   a. *Be* in all forms of the present tense.

   b. *Were* in all forms of the past tense.

   c. *Have been* in all forms of the present perfect tense.

9.3 VOICE

In general, use the active voice in writing. The passive voice should only be used when there are specific stylistic or contextual reasons.

A transitive verb is either active or passive. When the subject acts, the verb is active. Similarly, when the subject is acted upon, the verb is passive.

In writing, the active voice is preferable since it is emphatic and direct. A weak passive verb leaves the doer unknown or seemingly unimportant. The passive voice, however, is essential when the action of the verb is more important than the doer, when the doer is unknown, or when the writer wishes to place the emphasis on the receiver of the action rather than the doer.

Examples: Using the active voice rather than the passive.

   Weak Passive: The kitten was hit by the station wagon.

   Strong Active: The brown station wagon hit the kitten.

   Weak Passive: The members were questioned by the inter-
           viewer.

   Strong Active: The interviewer questioned the members.

Examples: Using the passive voice.

   Another man was hired yesterday.

Here, the action of the verb is more important than the

doer.

>*All the buildings were destroyed during the bombing.*
>
>*The girls were totally confused.*

In these examples, the emphasis is on the receiver of the verb.

9.4 EXERCISES

A. <u>FIGURES OF SPEECH</u> -- Write two sentences for each of the four figures of speech described.

B. <u>MOOD</u> -- Identify the mood in each of the following sentences.

   1. I hope that they arrive on time.
   2. Don't play with the radio or you will break it.
   3. Please, read the book.
   4. They have read that before.
   5. Is it time to go?

C. <u>MOOD</u> -- Choose the correct form of the verb given in parentheses in the following sentences.

   1. I demanded that the letter (be, is, was) sent special delivery.
   2. If Ann (were, was) at school yesterday, she (would, should) have received the notice.
   3. We (were, are) leaving when it began to rain.
   4. I realize that she (is, were) upset because of the outcome.
   5. If the teacher (were, is) here, you would have behaved.

D. <u>VOICE</u> -- In the following sentences, change the voice when necessary. Also, note the reason for the change.

   1. The brakes were not completely fixed by the garage repairman.
   2. The students are learning the necessity of basic writing skills.
   3. The campers were absolutely lost.
   4. The girl lost the spelling bee because she couldn't spell "conscious."
   5. The car crashed into the large oak tree during the rain storm.

CHAPTER 10

THE PARAGRAPH

After the sentence, the paragraph is the fundamental unit of communication. By organizing the main subject into smaller, more specific topics, the paragraph can focus on and develop these subjects more fully. A paragraph may be any length, although it is generally best not to write single sentences as full paragraphs. Usually, it requires <u>at least three</u> sentences to develop a topic to some degree. Most paragraphs are organized around a central idea. Each sentence must somehow relate to this idea or the paragraph will not cohere.

10.1 THE TOPIC SENTENCE

Usually, the first sentence tells the reader what the paragraph is about; it is called a <u>topic sentence</u>.

<u>Example</u>: The topic sentence for paragraph #1 is underlined.

> <u>*This fall, the freshman class at Oregon State felt the differences between high school and college tremendously.*</u> *Many were overwhelmed by the work load. In high school, for example, they were never required to read a hundred pages a night and then complete thirty questions. The freshman class also found the standards of their professors unusually high. Essays were expected to be neatly typed and proofread or they would not be accepted. Lastly, many students were not used to the responsibilities of living away from home. For many, it was the first time they had used a washing machine in eighteen years. Overall, freshman year at Oregon State was a trying time.*

The topic sentence for paragraph #2 is underlined.

> <u>*Yet the members of my sister's freshman class did not experience the same shock when they entered Oregon State four years ago.*</u> *It seems that in that short time, the stand-*

ards of the high schools have changed considerably. When my sister was a high school student, she was encouraged to achieve. The high school curriculum was also more academic. I can recall my sister and her friends studying late into the night. Furthermore, they never complained; they knew it was necessary to work hard. High school students no longer feel this way. This is only speculation, but I feel that the rigorous high school curriculum of the past not only prepared the freshman class at Oregon State academically, but also disciplined them and allowed them to handle better the added responsibility of college life.

Example: The topic sentence for paragraph #1 is underlined.

The film "Chariots of Fire" is much more than just a story of young runners. Throughout the film, running serves as a metaphor for absolute determination and belief. It is through running that the two athletes strengthen their own personal beliefs and build their self-confidence. The film is essentially about achieving the self-awareness necessary to reach a goal.

The topic sentence for paragraph #2 is underlined.

On the other hand, the film does communicate in depth the determination a runner must have if he is to succeed. In the film, there are many scenes that show the difficult training process, and the physical fitness necessary to compete in races. However, to be a winning athlete, absolute concentration and mental preparedness are also required. It is the combination of the two that makes a truly successful athlete.

Sometimes a writer may wish to emphasize a paragraph. A summarizing sentence at the end, along with the topic sentence in the beginning, frames the paragraph and draws attention to its details.

Example:

It was against all odds, but James managed to win the race. After being sidelined with injuries for half the season, James himself had given up on competing in the school marathon. His coach, however, encouraged him to train immediately after recovering. After weeks of training with little progress, James finally regained his concentration and began to make progress. Entering the race, he still wasn't expected to win. But not only did James win, he set a school record. It was an amazing victory.

A topic sentence, however, does not have to come at the beginning of a paragraph. Often it is found at the end, or occasionally in the middle. A writer should make a conscious decision about where the topic sentence is placed. At the beginning of a paragraph, it often captures the reader's interest and tells him what to expect. This is the form used in many magazine and newspaper articles for this very reason. At the end of a paragraph, the topic sentence can reinforce, or place emphasis on the details discussed within the paragraph. Compare the following paragraphs. In each, the topic sentence is underlined.

Example #1:

After the student protest Monday, the school board decided to reconsider its decision to raise tuition by 10% next year. Many students pointed to the fact that it would be nearly impossible to meet tuition costs because government loans and other forms of financial aid were being limited. A meeting will take place next week between the school board and the student representatives. They hope to reach a compromise.

Example #2:

We left early Saturday morning and arrived at the boat just before dawn as planned. It was a beautiful and sunny day; the sky was perfectly clear. Not only did I get a long needed tan, I actually caught five fish. It was a perfect day on the boat.

The topic sentence can influence and guide a reader. However, it should be equally important to the writer. Serving as a focus, only ideas which pertain to the topic sentence should be included in that particular paragraph. A writer should be careful not to include ideas or topics which are not clearly related. They should be developed in their own separate paragraph. Remember, in its most basic form, a piece of writing is composed of thoughts logically arranged. By referring back to the topic sentence, a writer can keep his work organized and consistent.

10.2 LINKING EXPRESSIONS AND CONNECTORS

A <u>coherent</u> paragraph or essay is not necessarily ensured because a writer arranges sentences logically. Linking expressions and connectors are crucial for smooth transitions between ideas and subjects. The links between paragraphs themselves can be made in many ways. Pronouns are often helpful for referring to a previous sentence without repetition. Conjunctions and certain adverbs are often used as transitions from paragraph to paragraph. Some that are frequently used are listed.

a. To elaborate on an idea already discussed, the following connectors are effective:

again	*furthermore*	*moreover*
also	*in addition*	*similarly*
and	*likewise*	*too*
for example		

<u>Examples</u>:

I intend to vote for John in the election next week. He is a diligent worker with a good personality. <u>Moreover</u>, he has experience in student government.

We feel it would be best to change the date of the picnic. Many members said they couldn't attend. <u>Also</u>, it is supposed to rain on that date.

I suggest you take the course on Russian literature. The material is interesting. <u>Furthermore</u>, the professor is liked by all his students.

b. To qualify, limit, or contradict a statement, use the following connectors:

but	*yet*	*although*
however	*nevertheless*	*on the other hand*
on the contrary		

<u>Examples</u>:

Mr. Brown thought he had secured the business deal.

All the necessary paperwork had been completed. <u>Yet</u> for some unknown reason, the company declined the of-fer at the last minute.

It looked as if the New York Yankees had lost an-other game. The Detroit Tigers were leading by seven runs after the fifth inning. <u>Nevertheless</u>, the Yankees came back to win the game by a score of 9-7.

After I located the problem, I thought I could fix the leak. I simply had to replace an old pipe. <u>However</u>, I didn't have the proper tools and a plumber had to be called to complete the job.

c. Connectors can also be used to show a time or a place arrangement of an idea. The following are often used:

at the present time	second	meanwhile
at the same time	finally	eventually
first	later	at this point
further		

<u>Examples:</u>

After going over the problem several times, I de-cided to ask my teacher for help. After she had ex-plained it fully, I looked the problem over one more time. <u>Finally</u>, I arrived at the correct solution.

We have been saving for many years for a trip to Europe. But each year, the plane fare increases and we realize we still don't have enough money. <u>Eventually</u>, we do expect to see Europe.

It was a hectic day. First, I missed the bus. Then, the subway was delayed for over an hour. When I finally reached home, it began to rain. <u>At this point</u>, I was about to cry.

d. The following connectors help to conclude a paragraph effectively:

as a result	hence
as can be seen	for these reasons
consequently	therefore

Examples:

The weatherman forcasted a blizzard for tomorrow. He expects the accumulation to be very heavy. Therefore, I decided to stock up on food items at the supermarket today.

After years of unfair taxation and abuse by England, the colonies decided to fight for their independence. The American Revolution succeeded, and British domination ended. Consequently, the colonists declared their independence and drafted a constitution to secure their rights in the future.

We were cautioned not to move if we heard voices. Suddenly something fell. As a result, no one moved an inch.

e. Pronouns are also effective connectors:

Examples:

Don't forget to read Shakespeare's Hamlet. That play is one of his best.

She likes many of your photographs. These are the ones she chose for the book.

I know that Jack would have agreed to the proposal. Not only is he a supporter of it, he was the one who made the suggestion in the first place.

These connectors should not be overused, or your writing will be awkward and monotonous. It is sometimes sufficient to merely repeat certain key words or ideas that have appeared in the preceding paragraph or line. The repetition of a subject-verb phrasing and parallel structure can also help to relate separate clauses and sentences.

Examples:

A noun is a word, a verb is a word. Sentences are collections of words. Paragraphs are collections of sentences.

Far overhead the stars were spinning. The earth was spinning, the moon was spinning. My head was spinning too, so when I looked at the road, it looked like everything was spinning.

The aim is to allow the reader to connect paragraphs and ideas in his mind. Occasionally, the line of argument may be so strong that an additional transition would be unnecessary. Deciding whether to use a connector or not is tricky, but largely a matter of common sense. The more you write, the easier it will be to decide. Also, try reading your work aloud. The ear often picks up many transitional problems.

10.3 EXPANDING A TOPIC SENTENCE INTO A PARAGRAPH

A topic sentence should be a statement of thesis. The remainder or body of the paragraph should clearly and completely prove this statement. Although there are many ways to develop a topic sentence into a paragraph, the use of detailed information is always necessary. Remember that these details must clearly relate to the topic sentence. The following are various ways of developing a topic sentence.

FACTS: Facts are often used to substantiate historical and scientific writing. In the exact sciences especially, facts are required.

EXAMPLES: In almost any kind of writing, examples help to clarify a statement. They offer the reader evidence.

ARGUMENT: In editorials, philosophical writing and literary criticism, for example, the argument is often used. Because these fields are not exact like the sciences, a well structured argument is needed to support a theory.

ANECDOTE: A short account of an incident, usually personal or bibliographical, often entertains the reader while clarifying a point. Anecdotes are often found in narrative writing.

DEFINITION: By defining a term or a concept, the writer often gives an explanation.

COMPARISON AND CONTRAST: By comparing and contrasting people, theories, etc., the essential qualities of the two are

ANALOGY:	In an analogy, something can be explained by comparing it point by point with something else. As in comparison and contrast, an analogy can bring out the essential qualities of a subject.
CAUSE AND EFFECT:	In scientific writing, a cause and effect relationship must be stated with accuracy. It usually involves the use of data. In other kinds of writing, cause and effect analysis can be made from more general observation.

The above are not simply ways of developing a topic sentence into a paragraph. When the development is carried through logically and thoroughly, this also helps the internal organization of the essay, by structuring and by giving the paragraphs coherence.

10.4 LACK OF UNITY IN A PARAGRAPH

A well written paragraph is unified. It is focused on one topic. If a second central idea is included, it produces a confusing result. Added ideas often enter into writing when a writer digresses or includes irrelevant details. In the following examples, the second topic is underlined.

NO: *The history of diving is quite interesting.*
George has always been fond of diving. When he was only seven, he was jumping from the high dive; at ten, he was a medalist on a diving team.

YES: *George has always been fond of diving. When he was only seven, he was jumping from the high dive; at ten, he was a medalist on a diving team.*

NO: *Even in the best of times, men can fail. It is a fact of the human condition that no-one's behavior is truly consistent. A person's intentions are very important. We mean well, do our best, and toss all our effort away in a moment.*

YES: *Even in the best of times, men can fail. It is a fact of the human condition that no-one's behavior is truly consistent. We mean well, do our best, and toss all our effort away in a moment.*

NO: My brother lives in Boston. He found a nice
big apartment on Commonwealth Avenue. *He likes
to read.* Although the landlord doesn't allow pets,
my brother has two cats. The cats seem to understand the situation, because they hide behind the
refrigerator whenever someone comes to the door.

YES: My brother lives in Boston. He found a nice,
big apartment on Commonwealth Avenue. Although
the landlord doesn't allow pets, he has two cats.
The cats seem to understand the situation, because
they hide behind the refrigerator whenever someone comes to the door.

NO: Were you at the party? I didn't see you there.
Clair's house is fairly large, but I'm still surprised
that I didn't see you. *I was wearing a new outfit.*

YES: Were you at the party? I didn't see you there.
Clair's house is fairly large, but I'm still surprised
that I didn't see you.

Again, by carefully proofreading and reading your writing
aloud, digressions and irrelevent details should become
obvious. Often these ideas can be omitted without having to
rewrite the paragraph.

10.5 LACK OF CONSISTENCY

In writing, consistency is as important as unity. Abrupt
changes in point of view and tone should be avoided. Point
of view is the place from which, or the way in which
something is viewed or considered; it is the writer's
standpoint. Point of view can also refer to the attitude a
writer has toward a subject. Tone, which is related to point
of view, is the manner of speaking which shows a certain
attitude. A particular tone such as informal, formal, or
dramatic, is achieved by word choice and phrasing.

10.5.1 POINT OF VIEW

NO: The old woman shuffled into the room, her
eyes glued to the floor. Her clothes were carefully chosen; they were her very best. Some-

one coughed nervously, and a chair scraped the floor. *I think it was Mr. Ohlsen's chair.*

YES: The old woman shuffled into the room, her eyes glued to the floor. Her clothes were carefully chosen; they were her very best. Someone coughed nervously and a chair, probably Mr. Ohlsen's, scraped the floor.

NO: Mary held the papers tightly in her hand. "Let me see those," the teacher demanded, and beckoned with a grasping motion. *We knew that the papers were notes meant for Charles,* and the teacher probably guessed that too.

YES: Mary held the papers tightly in her hand. "Let me see those," the teacher demanded, and beckoned with a grasping motion. The papers were notes meant for Charles, and the teacher probably knew it.

NO: From the pool Jerry could see the men enter the house. They broke the lock on the front door, and went in that way. After that, he lost sight of them. *His wife saw everything from the top of the stairs.*

YES: From the pool Jerry could see the men enter the house. They broke the lock on the front door, and went in that way. Although Jerry lost sight of them at this point, his wife was inside and saw everything.

10.5.2 TONE

NO: At a special press conference at the White House today, the president offered reporters details of his new economic policy. Hoping to lower inflation and unemployment, he proposed a series of tax cuts that will be made over the next three years. Many economists believe *it's about time the president did something.*

YES: At a special press conference at the White House today, the president offered reporters details of his new economic policy. Hoping to lower inflation and unemployment, he proposed a series of tax cuts that will be made over the next three *years. Many economists believe it is a good time for the president to implement his new plan.*

NO: *At work today, I received a message that my cousins from Mississippi were arriving on the seven o'clock train, a day earlier than expected. Luckily, I was wearing an outfit that I could greet them in. All that I needed to do was pick up a few items at the supermarket. It seemed that everthing was under control. But alas, that clumsy fool at the cash register dropped my packages carelessly to the ground. As a result, I had to shop all over again.*

YES: *At work today, I received a message that my cousins from Mississippi were arriving on the seven o'clock train, a day earlier than expected. Luckily, I was wearing an outfit that I could greet them in. All that I needed to do was pick up a few items at the supermarket. It seemed that everything was under control. The cashier, however, carelessly dropped my packages. As a result, I had to shop all over again.*

NO: *Giving my neighbor instructions for the pie crust, she mixed the flour and the shortening with the water and then proceded to knead the dough with the utmost care and patience for five minutes.*

YES: *Giving my neighbor instructions for the pie crust, she mixed the flour and the shortening with the water and then carefully kneaded the dough for five minutes.*

Perhaps the key word in writing a paragraph and ultimately an essay is focus. This is actually what has been stressed throughout this chapter. That is why the topic sentence is such an important element. Problems of clarity, unity, repetition and consistency rarely occur when a writer has clearly defined his subject. But focus in writing does not come from merely researching a topic. Writing is a thoughtful process. Where there is understanding, a focus cannot help but develop.

10.6 EXERCISES

A. The following topics can be developed into paragraphs. Choose five and write a topic sentence for each. From these five, expand three of your topic sentences into well developed paragraphs.

1. Your most memorable day
2. Nuclear energy
3. A hero
4. The quality of your education
5. The voting age
6. Living away from home
7. Your most embarrassing moment
8. Being a conformist or a radical
9. Your favorite sport
10. Winning a contest

Take one of the paragraphs you have just written and revise it by drastically changing its <u>tone</u>. Make the tone formal, humorous, or dramatic, for example.

B. Write four paragraphs using four of the methods that follow. Listed below are also some suggestions for topics.

1. facts
2. examples
3. argument
4. anecdote

5. definition
6. comparison and contrast
7. analogy
8. cause and effect

1. Facts--Using facts substantiate a case for the banning of cigarettes.

2. Examples-- Using examples illustrate the success or lack of success of a president's administration.

3. Argument--Support your stand on the death penalty (or some other controversial issue) by using an argument.

4. Anecdote--Using Ralph Waldo Emerson's quote "The revelation of thought takes man from servitude into freedom," write an anecdote.

10.6 EXERCISES

5. <u>Comparison and Contrast</u>--Compare and contrast two historical figures.

6. <u>Analogy</u>-- Compare a family member with an animal.

7. <u>Cause and Effect</u>--Show a cause and effect relationship between your grades and your study habits.

Now proofread the four paragraphs you have written. Underline the linking expressions and connectors you have used, adding any that are necessary.

C. <u>POINT OF VIEW</u>:

Skim through a magazine or a newspaper. Select three articles and define the author's point of view, his attitudes, the time and the place. Also note how the language and the use of punctuation contributes to the point of view. Does the author change his point in the article? If so, why?

D. In the following paragraphs make the necessary revisions.

1.   At the year end meeting of the Key Club, the president summarized the events and the activities of the past year. He also remarked on the success of the annual fund raiser. The dance marathon raised five hundred dollars for underprivileged children. We were all pleased when we learned this.

2.   The teacher handed out the final examinations. He cautioned us to read the directions carefully. All essays had to be legible and grammatically correct or they would not be accepted. We couldn't wait to get to it.

3.   Thomas Hobbes is the author of <u>The Leviathan</u>. He was born in England in 1588. In the book, Hobbes states that men are radically and aggressively selfish, yet manage to live in an ordered state. His premise leads him to justify this formation of State. Every individual must be willing, in exchange for security, to abandon his natural liberty to do as he likes, and be contented with so much liberty as he would be willing to give others.

CHAPTER 11

PUNCTUATION

Try to read this paragraph:

take some more tea the march hare said to alice very earnestly ive had nothing yet alice replied in an offended tone so i cant take more you mean you cant take less said the hatter its very easy to take more than nothing lewis carroll

Now try again:

> *"Take some more tea," the March Hare said to Alice, very earnestly.*
> *"I've had nothing yet," Alice replied in an offended tone, "so I can't take more."*
> *"You mean you can't take less," said the Hatter, "it's very easy to take more than nothing."*

> *--Lewis Carroll*

This example illustrates how much punctuation helps the reader understand what the writer is trying to say. The most important role of punctuation is clarification.

In speech, words are accompanied by gesture, voice, tone and rhythm that help convey a desired meaning. In writing, it is punctuation alone that must do the same job.

There are many rules about how to use the various punctuation marks. These are sometimes difficult to understand because they are described with so much grammatical terminology. Therefore, this discussion of punctuation will avoid as much terminology as possible. If you still find the rules confusing, and your method of punctuation is somewhat random, try to remember that most punctuation takes the place of pauses in speech.

Keeping this in mind, it is helpful to read your sentences aloud as you write; if you punctuate according to the pauses in your voice, you will do much better than if you put in your commas, periods and dashes at random, or where they look good.

11.1 STOPS

There are three ways to end a sentence:

1. a period
2. a question mark
3. an exclamation point

11.1.1 THE PERIOD

Periods end all sentences that are not questions or exclamations. In speech, the end of a sentence is indicated with a full pause. The period is the counterpart of this pause in writing:

Go get me my paper. I'm anxious to see the news.

Into each life some rain must fall. Last night some fell into mine.

The moon is round. The stars look small.

Mary and Janet welcomed the newcomer. She was noticeably happy.

When a question is intended as a suggestion and the listener is not expected to answer, or when a question is asked indirectly as part of a sentence, a period is also used:

Mimi wondered if the parade would ever end.

May we hear from you soon.

Will you please send the flowers you advertised.

We'll never know who the culprit was.

Periods also follow most abbreviations and contractions:

N.Y.	*Dr.*	*Jr.*	*Sr.*
etc.	*Jan.*	*Mrs.*	*Mr.*

| _Esq._ | _cont._ | _A.M._ | _A.D._ |

Periods (or parentheses) are also used after a letter or number in a series:

a. apples	_1. president_
b. oranges	_2. vice president_
c. pears	_3. secretary_

<u>Errors to Avoid</u>

Be sure to omit the period after a quotation mark preceded by a period. Only one stop is necessary to end a sentence:

She said, "Hold my hand." (no period after the final ")

"Don't go into the park until later."

"It's not my fault," he said. "She would have taken the car anyway."

After many abbreviations, particularly for organizations or agencies, no period is used (check your dictionary if in doubt):

AFL–CIO	_NAACP_	_GM_
FBI	_NATO_	_IBM_
_TV_	_UN_	_HEW_

11.1.2 THE QUESTION MARK

Use a question mark to end a direct question even if it is not in the form of a question. The question mark in writing is the same as the rising tone of voice used to indicate a question in speech. If you read the following two sentences aloud, you will see the difference in tone between a statement and a question composed of the same words.

Mary is here.

Mary is here?

Here are some more examples of correct use of question marks; pay special attention to the way they are used with other punctuation:

Where will we go next?

> *Would you like coffee or tea?*
>
> *"Won't you," he asked, "please lend me a hand?"*
>
> *"Will they ever give us our freedom?" the prisoner asked.*
>
> *"To be or not to be?" was the question asked by Hamlet.*
>
> *Who asked "When?"*

Question marks indicate a full stop and lend a different emphasis to a sentence than do commas. Compare these pairs of sentences:

> *Was the sonata by Beethoven? or Brahms? or Chopin?*
>
> *Was the sonata by Beethoven, or Brahms, or Chopin?*
>
> *Did they walk to the park? climb the small hill? take the bus to town? or go skating out back?*
>
> *Did they walk to town, climb the small hill, take the bus to town, or go skating out back?*

Sometimes question marks are placed in parentheses. This indicates doubt or uncertainty about the facts being reported:

> *The bombing started at 3:00 A.M. (?)*
>
> *She said the dress cost 200,000 (?) dollars.*
>
> *Harriet Stacher (18 (?)-1914) was well thought of in her time.*
>
> *Hippocrates (460 (?) - (?) 377 B.C.) is said to be the father of modern medicine.*

11.1.3 THE EXCLAMATION POINT

An exclamation point ends an emphatic statement. It should be used only to express strong emotions such as surprise, disbelief, or admiration. If it is used too often for mild expressions of emotion, it loses its effectiveness.

> *Let go of me!*
>
> *Help! Fire!*

It was a wonderful day!

What a beautiful woman she is!

Who shouted "Fire!" (notice no question mark is necessary)

Fantastic!

"Unbelievable!" she gasped. (notice no comma is necessary)

"You'll never win!" he cried.

Where else can I go! (The use of the exclamation point shows that this is a strong <u>statement</u> even though it is <u>worded</u> <u>like</u> a question.)

<u>Avoid Overuse</u>

The following is an example of the overuse of exclamation points:

Dear Susan,

 I was so glad to see you last week! You looked better than ever! Our talk meant so much to me! I can hardly wait until we get together again! Could you believe how long it has been! Let's never let that happen again! Please write as soon as you get the chance! I can hardly wait to hear from you!

        Your friend,

        Nora

11.1.3.1 INTERJECTIONS

An interjection is a word or group of words used as an exclamation to express emotion. It need not be followed by an exclamation point. Often an interjection is followed by a comma (see "THE COMMA") if it is not very intense. Technically, the interjection has no grammatical relation to other words in the sentence, yet it is still considered a part of speech.

<u>Examples:</u>

<u>*Oh dear*</u>*, I forgot my keys again.*

<u>*Ah!*</u> *Now do you understand?*

Ouch! I didn't realize that the stove was hot.

Oh, excuse me. I didn't realize that you were next on line.

11.2 PAUSES

There are five ways to indicate a pause shorter than a period:

1. dash
2. colon
3. parentheses
4. semicolon
5. comma

11.2.1 THE DASH

Use the dash to indicate a sudden or unexpected break in the normal flow of the sentence. It can also be used in the place of parentheses or of commas if the meaning is clarified. Usually the dash gives the material it sets off special emphasis. (On a typewriter, two hyphens (--) indicate a dash.)

Could you--I hate to ask!--help me with these boxes?

When we left town--a day never to be forgotten--they had a record snowfall.

She said--we all heard it--"The safe is not locked."

These are the three ladies--Mrs. Jackson, Miss Harris and Ms. Forrester--you hoped to meet last week.

The sight of the Andromeda Galaxy--especially when seen for the first time--is astounding.

That day was the longest in her life--or so it seemed to her.

A dash is often used to summarize a series of ideas that have already been expressed:

Freedom of speech, freedom to vote and freedom of assembly--these are the cornerstones of democracy.

> *Carbohydrates, fats and proteins--these are the basic kinds of food we need.*

> *Jones, who first suggested we go; Marshall, who made all the arrangements; and Kline, who finally took us there-- these were the three men I admired most for their courage.*

> *James, Howard, Marianne, Angela, Catherine--all were displeased with the decision of the teacher.*

The dash is also used to note the author of a quotation that is set off in the text:

> *Nothing is good or bad but thinking makes it so.*
>
> *--William Shakespeare*

> *Under every grief and pine Runs a joy with silken twine.*
>
> *--William Blake*

11.2.2 THE COLON

The colon (:) is the sign of a pause about midway in length between the semicolon and the period. It can often be replaced by a comma and sometimes by a period. Although used less frequently now than it was 50 to 75 years ago, the colon is still convenient to use, for it signals to the reader that more information is to come on the subject of concern. The colon can also create a slight dramatic tension.

It is used to introduce a word, phrase or complete statement (clause) that emphasizes, illustrates or exemplifies what has already been stated:

> *He had only one desire in life: to play baseball.*

> *The weather that day was the most unusual I'd ever seen: It snowed and rained while the sun was still shining.*

> *In his speech, the president surprised us by his final point: the conventional grading system would be replaced next year.*

> *Jean thought of only two things the last half hour of the hike home: a bath and a bed.*

Notice that the word following the colon can start with either a capital or a small letter. Use a capital letter if the word following the colon begins another complete sentence. But when the words following the colon are part of the sentence preceding the colon, use a small letter.

> *May I offer your a suggestion: don't drive without your seatbelts fastened.*

> *The thought continued to perplex him: Where will I go next?*

When introducing a series that illustrates or emphasizes what has already been stated, use the colon:

> *Only a few of the graduates were able to be there: Jamison, Mearns, Linkley and Commoner.*

> *For Omar Khayyam, a Persian poet, three things are necessary for a paradise on earth: a loaf of bread, a jug of wine, and his beloved.*

> *In the basement, he kept some equipment for his experiments: the test tubes, some chemical agents, three sunlamps, and the drill.*

Long quotes set off from the rest of the text by indentation rather than quotation marks are generally introduced with a colon:

> *The first line of Lincoln's Gettysburg address is familiar to most Americans:*

> > *Fourscore and seven years ago our fathers brought forth on this continent a new nation, conceived in liberty and dedicated to the proposition that all men are created equal.*

> *I quote from Shakespeare's* Sonnets*:*

> > *When I do count the clock that tells the time,*
> > *And see the brave day sunk in hideous night;*
> > *When I behold the violet past prime,*
> > *And sable curls all silver'd o'er with white...*

It is also customary to begin a business letter with a colon:

> *Dear Senator Jordan:*

> *To Whom It May Concern:*

> *Gentlemen:*

> *Dear Sir or Madam:*

But in informal letters, use a comma:

Dear Mary,

Dear Father,

The colon is also used in introducing a list:

Please send the following:

    1. 50 index cards,
    2. 4 typewriter ribbons,
    3. 8 erasers.

Prepare the recipe as follows:

    1. Slice the oranges thinly.
    2. Arrange them in a circle around the straw -
        berries.
    3. Pour the liqueur over both fruits.

At least three ladies will have to be there to help:

    1. Mrs. Goldman, who will greet the guests;
    2. Harriet Sacher, who will serve the lunch; and
    3. my sister, who will do whatever else needs
        to be done.

Finally, the colon is used between numbers when writing the time, between the volume and number or volume and page number of a journal and also between the chapter and verse in the Bible.

4:30 P.M.

The Nation, 34:8

Genesis 5:18

11.2.3 PARENTHESES

To set off material that is only loosely connected to the central meaning of the sentence, use parentheses [()]:

Most men (at least, most that I know) like wine, women and song, but have too much work and not enough time for such enjoyments.

On Tuesday evenings and Thursday afternoons (the times I don't have classes), the television programs are not too exciting.

*Last year at Vale (we go there every year), the skiing
was the best I've ever seen.*

*In New York (I've lived there all my life and ought to
know), you have to have a license for a gun.*

*What must be done to think clearly and calmly (is it even
possible?) and then make the decision?*

Watch out for other punctuation when you use parentheses.
Punctuation that refers to the material enclosed in the
parentheses occurs inside the marks. Punctuation belonging
to the rest of the sentence comes outside the parentheses.

I thought I knew the poem by heart (boy, was I wrong!).

*For a long time (too long as far as I'm concerned), women
were thought to be inferior to men.*

*We must always strive to tell the truth. (Are we even
sure we know what truth is?)*

*When I first saw a rose (don't you think it's the most
beautiful flower?), I thought it must be man-made.*

11.2.4 THE SEMICOLON

Semicolons (;) are sometimes called mild periods. They
indicate a pause midway in length between the comma and
the colon. Writing that contains many semicolons is usually in
a dignified, formal style. To use them correctly, it is
necessary to be able to recognize main clauses--complete
ideas. When two main clauses occur in a single sentence
without a connecting word (*and*, *but*, *or*, *nor*, *for*), the
appropriate mark of punctuation is the semicolon.

*It is not a good idea for you to leave the country right
now; you should actually try to stay as long as you pos-
sibly can.*

Music lightens life; literature deepens it.

*In the past, boy babies were often dressed in blue; girls
in pink.* ("were often dressed" is understood in the
second part of the sentence.)

*Can't you see it's no good to go on alone; we'll starve
to death if we keep traveling this way much longer.*

*Burgundy and maroon are very similar colors; scarlet
is altogether different.*

Notice how the use of the comma, period and semicolon each gives a sentence a slightly different meaning:

Music lightens life; literature deepens it.

Just as music lightens life, literature deepens it.

Music lightens life. Literature deepens it.

The semicolon lends a certain balance to writing that would otherwise be difficult to achieve. Nonetheless, you should be careful not to overuse it. A comma can just as well join parts of a sentence with two main ideas; the semicolon is particularly appropriate if there is a striking contrast in the two ideas expressed:

*Ask not what your country can do for you; ask what
you can do for your country.*

*It started out as an ordinary day; it ended being the
most extraordinary of her life.*

*Our power to apprehend truth is limited; to seek it,
limitless.*

If any one of the following words or phrases are used to join together compound sentences, they are generally preceded by a semicolon:

then	*however*	*thus*	*furthermore*
hence	*indeed*	*so*	*consequently*
also	*that is*	*yet*	*nevertheless*
anyhow	*in addition*	*in fact*	*on the other hand*
likewise	*moreover*	*still*	*meanwhile*
instead	*besides*	*otherwise*	*in other words*
henceforth	*for example*	*therefore*	*at the same time*
even now			

*For a long time, people thought that women were inferior
to men; <u>even now</u> it is not an easy attitude to overcome.*

*Being clever and cynical, he succeeded in becoming
president of the company; <u>meanwhile</u> , his wife left him.*

*Cigarette smoking has never interested me; <u>furthermore,</u>
I couldn't care less if anyone else smokes or not.*

Some say Bach was the greatest composer of all time; <u>yet</u> he still managed to have an ordinary life in other ways: he and his wife had 20 children.

We left wishing we could have stayed much longer; <u>in other words</u>, they showed us a good time.

When a series of complicated items are listed or if there is internal punctuation in a series, the semicolon is sometimes used to make the meaning more clear:

You can use your new car for many things: to drive to town or to the country; to impress your friends and neighbors; to protect yourself from rain on a trip away from home; and to borrow against should you need money right away.

The scores from yesterday's games came in late last night: Pirates-6, Zoomers-3; Caterpillars-12, Steelys-8; Crashers-9, Links-8; and Greens-15, Uptowns-4.

In October a bag of potatoes cost 69¢; in December 99¢; in February $1.09; in April $1.39. I wonder if this inflation will ever stop.

The semicolon is placed outside quotation marks or parentheses, unless it is a part of the material enclosed in those marks.

I used to call him "my lord and master"; it made him laugh every time.

The weather was cold for that time of year (I was shivering wherever I went); nevertheless, we set out to hike to the top of that mountain.

11.2.5 THE COMMA

Of all the marks of punctuation, the comma (,) has the most uses. Before you tackle the main principles that guide its usage, be sure that you have an elementary understanding of sentence structure. There are actually only a few rules and conventions to follow when using commas; the rest is common sense. The worst abuse of commas comes from those who overuse them, who place them illogically. If you are ever in doubt as to whether or not to use a comma, do not use it.

11.2.5.1 IN A SERIES

When more than one adjective (an adjective series) describes a noun, use a comma to separate and emphasize each adjective.

> *the long, dark passageway*
>
> *another confusing, sleepless night*
>
> *a healthy, young girl*
>
> *the bright, red dog*
>
> *an elaborate, complex plan*
>
> *the beautiful, starry night*
>
> *the haunting, melodic sound*
>
> *the old, grey, crumpled hat*

In these instances, the comma takes the place of "and". To test if the comma is needed, try inserting "and" between the adjectives in question. If it is logical, you should use a comma. The following are examples of adjectives that describe an adjective-noun combination that has come to be thought of almost as one word. In such cases the adjective in front of the adjective-noun combination needs no comma.

> *a stately oak tree*   *my worst report card*
>
> *an exceptional wine glass*   *a borrowed record player*
>
> *a successful garage sale*   *a porcelain dinner plate*

If you insert "and" between the adjectives in the above examples, it will not make sense.

The comma is also used to separate words, phrases and whole ideas (clauses); it still takes the place of "and" when used this way:

> *an apple, a pear, a fig, and a banana*
>
> *a lovely lady, an indecent dress, and many admirers*
>
> *She lowered the shade, closed the curtain, turned off the light, and went to bed.*
>
> *John, Frank, and my Uncle Harry all thought it was a questionable theory.*

The only question that exists about the use of commas in a series is whether or not one should be used before the final item. Usually "and" or "or" precedes the final item, and many writers do not include the comma before the final "and" or "or." When first learning, however, it is advisable to use the comma because often its omission can be confusing; in such cases as these, for instance:

> NO: *Would you like to shop at Sak's, Lord and Taylor's and Gimbels?*

> NO: *He got on his horse, tracked a rabbit and a deer and rode on to Canton.*

> NO: *We planned the trip with Mary and Harold, Susan, Dick and Joan, Gregory and Jean and Charles.*
> (Is it Gregory and Jean or Jean and Charles or Gregory and Jean and Charles?)

11.2.5.2 WITH A LONG INTRODUCTORY PHRASE

Usually if a phrase of more than five or six words precedes the subject at the beginning of a sentence, a comma is used to set it off.

> *After last night's fiasco at the disco, she couldn't bear the thought of looking at him again.*

> *Whenever I try to talk about politics, my husband leaves the room.*

> *When it comes to actual facts, every generation makes the same mistakes as the preceding one.*

> *Provided you have said nothing, they will never guess who you are.*

It is not necessary to use a comma with a short phrase:

> *In January she will go to Switzerland.*

> *After I rest I'll feel better.*

> *At Grandma's we had a big dinner.*

> *During the day no one is home.*

Sometimes a short introductory phrase is set off with a comma for emphasis, but usually it is better to leave the comma out.

> *At midnight, you'll be there, won't you?*

If an introductory phrase includes a verb form that is being used as another part of speech (a "verbal"), it must be followed by a comma. Try to make sense of the following sentences without commas.

NO: *When eating Mary never looked up from her plate.*

(When eating, Mary never looked up from her plate.)

NO: *Because of her desire to follow her faith in James wavered.*
(Because of her desire to follow, her faith in James wavered.)

NO: *Having decided to leave Mary James wrote her a letter.*
(Having decided to leave Mary, James wrote her a letter.)

Above all, common sense is the best guideline when trying to decide whether or not to use a comma after an introductory phrase. Does the comma make the meaning more clear? If it does, use it; if not, there is no reason to insert it.

11.2.5.3 TO SEPARATE SENTENCES WITH TWO MAIN IDEAS (COMPOUND SENTENCES)

To understand this use of the comma, you need to have studied sentence structure and be able to recognize compound sentences.

When a sentence contains more than two subjects and verbs (clauses) and the two clauses are joined by a connecting word *(and, but, or, yet, for, nor)*, use a comma before the connecting word to show that another clause is coming.

I thought I knew the poem by heart, but he showed me three lines I had forgotten.

Are we really interested in helping the children, or are we more concerned with protecting our good names?

He is supposed to leave tomorrow, but who knows if he will be ready to go.

Jim knows you are disappointed, and he has known it for a long time.

Living has its good points to be sure, yet I will not mind when it is over.

If the two parts of the sentence are short and closely

related, it is not necessary to use a comma:

> *He threw the ball and the dog ran after it.*

> *Jane played the piano and Charles danced.*

Errors to Avoid

Be careful not to confuse a sentence that has a compound verb and a single subject with a compound sentence. If the subject is the same for both verbs, there is no need for a comma:

> NO: *Charles sent some flowers, and wrote a long letter explaining why he had not been able to come.*

> NO: *Last Thursday we went to the concert with Julia, and afterwards dined at an old Italian restaurant.*

> NO: *For the third time, the teacher explained that the literacy level of high school students was much lower than it had been in previous years, and, this time, wrote the statistics on the board for everyone to see.*

11.2.5.4 TO SET OFF INTERRUPTING MATERIAL

There are so many different kinds of interruptions that can occur in a sentence that a list of them all would be quite lengthy. In general, words and phrases that stop the flow of the sentence or are unnecessary for the main idea are set off by commas. Some examples are:

Abbreviations after names:

Did you invite John Paul, Jr., and his sister?

Martha Harris, Ph.D., will be the speaker tonight.

Interjections: An exclamation added without grammatical connection.

Oh, I'm so glad to see you.

I tried so hard, alas, to do it.

Hey, let me out of here.

No, I will not let you out.

Direct address:

Roy, won't you open the door for the dog?

I can't understand, mother, what you are trying to say.

May I ask, Mr. President, why you called us together?

Hey, lady, watch out for the car!

Tag questions: A question that repeats the helping verb in a negative phrase.

I'm really hungry, aren't you?

Jerry looks like his father, doesn't he?

You'll come early, won't you?

We are expected at nine, aren't we?

Mr. Jones can chair the meeting, can't he?

Geographical names and addresses:

The concert will be held in Chicago, Illinois, on August 12.

They visited Tours, France, last summer.

The letter was addressed to Ms. Marion Heartwell, 1881 Pine Lane, Palo Alto, California 95824.
(No comma is needed before the zip code because it is already clearly set off from the state name.

Transitional words and phrases:

On the other hand, I hope he gets better.

In addition, the phone rang six times this afternoon.

I'm, nevertheless, going to the beach on Sunday.

You'll find, therefore, no one more loyal to me than you.

To tell the truth, I don't know what to believe.

Parenthetical words and phrases:

You will become, I believe, a great statesman.

We know, of course, that this is the only thing to do.

In fact, I planted corn last summer.

The Mannes affair was, to put it mildly, a surprise.

Bathing suits, generally speaking, are getting smaller.

<u>Unusual word order</u>:

The dress, new and crisp, hung in the closet. (Normal word order: The new crisp dress hung in the closet.)

To me, come softly and gently. (Normal word order: Come to me sofly and gently.)

Intently, she stared out the window. (Normal word order: She stared intently out the window.)

11.2.5.5 NONRESTRICTIVE ELEMENTS (NOT ESSENTIAL TO THE MEANING)

Parts of a sentence that modify other parts are sometimes essential to the meaning of the sentence and sometimes not. When a modifying word or group of words is not vital to the meaning of the sentence, it is set off by commas. Since it does not restrict the meaning of the words it modifies, it is called "nonrestrictive." Modifiers that are essential to the meaning of the sentence are called "restrictive" and are not set off by commas. Compare the following pairs of sentences:

The girl <u>who wrote the story</u> is my sister. (essential)

My sister, <u>the girl who wrote the story</u>, has always been drawn to adventure. (nonessential)

John Milton's famous poem <u>"Paradise Lost"</u> tells a remarkable story. (essential--Milton has written other poems)

Dante's great work, <u>"The Divine Comedy"</u>, marked the beginning of the Renaissance and the end of the Dark Ages. (nonessential--Dante wrote only one great work)

The cup <u>that is on the piano</u> is the one I want. (essential)

The cup, <u>which my brother gave me last year</u>, is on the piano. (nonessential)

My parakeet <u>Simian</u> has an extensive vocabulary. (essential--because there are no commas, the writer must have more than one parakeet)

My parakeet, <u>Simian</u>, has an extensive vocabulary. (nonessential--the writer must have only one parakeet whose name is Simian)

The people <u>who arrived late</u> were not seated. (essential)

George, <u>who arrived late</u>, was not seated. (nonessential)

She always listened to her sister <u>Jean</u>. (essential--she must have more than one sister)

She always listened to her husband, <u>Jack</u>. (nonessential--obviously, she has only one husband)

11.2.5.6 TO SET OFF DIRECT QUOTATIONS

Most direct quotes or quoted materials are set off from the rest of the sentence by commas:

"Please read your part more loudly," the director insisted.

"I won't know what to do," said Michael, "if you leave me now."

The teacher said sternly, "I will not dismiss this class until I have silence."

Mark looked up from his work, smiled, and said, "We'll be with you in a moment."

Be careful not to set off indirect quotations or quotes that are used as subjects or complements:

"To be or not to be" is the famous beginning of a soliloquy in Shakespeare's <u>Hamlet</u>. (subject)

Back then my favorite song was "A Summer Place." (complement)

She said she would never come back. (indirect quote)

"Place two tablespoons of chocolate in this pan." were her first words to her apprentice in the kitchen. (subject)

11.2.5.7 TO SET OFF CONTRASTING ELEMENTS

Her intelligence, <u>not her beauty</u>, got her the job.

Your plan will take you further from, <u>rather than closer to,</u> your destination.

It was a reasonable, <u>though not appealing</u>, idea.

He wanted glory, <u>but found happiness instead</u>.

James wanted an active, <u>not a passive</u>, partner.

11.2.5.8 IN DATES

(Both forms of the date are acceptable.)

She will arrive on April 6, 1981.
He left on 5 December 1980.
In January, 1967, he handed in his resignation.
In January 1967 he handed in his resignation.

11.3 EXERCISES

A. In the following sentences correctly supply periods, question marks, and exclamation points.

1. "Good gracious " she said "Didn't you know that I was coming "

2. Mr. Morgan works for the CIA

3. Alexander wondered if it was time to go

4. Leave me alone Can't you see that I'm busy

5. "How many boxes did you buy " asked Dr. Jones

6. "Be careful" he shouted "Didn't you see the car coming "

7. Impossible I have never seen anything like that before

8. Lynn asked if anyone had the time

9. What else can I do I lost all my money

10. Who cried "Help"

B. In the following sentences insert commas wherever necessary. You may also want to note the reason for your choice.

1. However I am willing to reconsider.

2. She descended the long winding staircase.

3. Whenever I practice the violin my family closes the windows .

4. While driving Francis never took his eyes off the road.

5. The car which I bought last year is in the garage .

6. "Answer the door" said his mother loudly .

7. Miss can I ask you for the time?

8. He was after all an ex-convict .

9. I'm so bored aren't you?

10. The old tall shady tree is wonderful during the summer.

11. George Gary and Bill were on line early this morning. They bought their tickets read the newspaper and spoke for a while.

12. The author James Grey was awarded the prize.

13. She attended school in London England last year.

14. They said they would do the job.

11.3 EXERCISES

15. His weight not his height prevented him from competing in the race.

16. The family who won the lottery lives in New Jersey.

17. She got in the car turned on the ignition and left the curb.

18. Incidentally he called last night.

19. The kitten small and cute was adopted by the Brown family.

20. Mary did you see James Jr. at the party last night?

21. Lisa saw the mailman and gave him the letter.

22. Last night I finished my essay and started on my next assignment.

23. Really I can't believe that is the truth.

24. We thought it was time to leave but we arrived early.

25. Monday she will leave for Boston.

26. After he got home he read a magazine ate dinner and left for the movies.

27. If you pass the test you will graduate.

28. When she decided to leave everyone was disappointed.

29. Hey John it's time to go.

30. He seemed wrong for the part yet he turned out to be the best actor in the production.

C. Correctly place the colon and the semicolon in the following sentences.

1. I have only one thing to say don't do it.

2. They seemed compatible yet they did not get along.

3. She had only one goal in life to be a famous pianist.

4. He thought the problem was solved instead his solution proved to be entirely wrong.

5. By the end of the day there were only two things on her mind rest and relaxation.

6. Only a few members were able to attend the convention Henry, Karen, David, Mark and Susan.

7. They were willing to accept the proposal he was not.

8. The art students were expected to supply the following brushes, paints, pallets and pads.

11.3 EXERCISES

9. The time is now the time is right.

10. The highest scores on the final exam are as follows Linda Jones 96 John Smith 94 Susan Green 90. These grades are unusually high they must have studied well.

D. Read the following sentences. What effect does the dash have on the writing, especially the tone and mood.

1. Can you?--I would be ever so grateful--I'm having so much difficulty.

2. Could it be--no it can't be--not after all these years.

3. Time and patience--two simple words--yet why are they so hard for me to remember.

4. Most of the paintings in the gallery--in fact all but one-- were done in the 19th century.

5. According to John Locke, these are man's inalienable rights-- life, liberty and property.

E. Read the following sentences. What effect does the use of parentheses have on the writing? Also make any necessary corrections.

1. The choice (in my opinion,) was a good one.

2. Linda's comment ("Where did you get that dress")? wasn't intended to be sarcastic.

3. After today (and what a day it was!) I will begin to work harder.

4. Last summer in Cape Cod (this is the first year we went there,) we did a lot of sightseeing.

5. The first time I went driving (do you remember the day)?, I was so scared.

ALL OF THE NEEDED PUNCTUATION AND OTHER ASPECTS OF MECHANICS HAVE BEEN OMITTED FROM THE FOLLOWING PASSAGE. IN MAKING THE NECESSARY CORRECTIONS THERE WILL OFTEN BE MORE THAN ONE WAY OF CORRECTING THE ERROR. THEREFORE, TRY TAKING INTO ACCOUNT THE MOOD AND TONE OF THE WRITING AND THE OVERALL COHERENCE OF THE PIECE WHEN PUNCTUATING THE PASSAGE.

11.3 EXERCISES

my sister amy had finally finished packing for college at about 11 am what a day it was as usual she had overpacked but this was clearly an understatement standing in the hall way were the following 7 large blue suitcases 3 borrowed trunks 4 old bulging macys shopping bags and 2 duffel bags but im going halfway across the united states how many times do you think ill be coming home she asked once every 5 years at christmas time i guessed i do hope youll write seriously do you know the difference between the words pack and hoard i said amy laughed self-consciously civilization does exist in chicago illinois i added trust me it really does really remarked amy with her own personal brand of sarcasm after all its only the 1980s its well known that 3 4 s of chicago is still unsettled territory i turned away in disgust it was useless

i went to help amy with her baggage picking up the large over stuffed green duffel bag i screamed whats in here is this a 50 or 100 pound bag you have got to be kidding i added she had filled the entire bag with books i knew shed want to take a couple of her favorite books and magazines albert camus the stranger charles dickens great expectations shakespeares king lear copies of keats and ts eliots best poems some national geographics but i realized i was all wrong instead she had packed 30 copies of tolstoys war and peace or so it seemed on her book shelf remained 1 lone copy of websters new collegiate dictionary in fact it was an extra one she had received it for her birthday last year i believe the rest of the move was sadly repetitious i realized amy was nuts

i wasnt about to reason with her i was tired it was futile there was no time meanwhile amy was totally calm and relaxed as she went through the radio stations finally settling on wnbc as she listened to the beatles hey jude i seemingly all powerful carried the last trunk out the door the plane a 747 was scheduled to leave at 12 oclock we were 10 minutes off schedule when we arrived at kennedy airport furthermore i had to pay a $5.00 surcharge for the extra baggage amy said she only had large bills as she was about to board the plane after 101 good byes i handed her a package as if she really needed anything else its a green pull over sweater just like mine i said tearfully oh you really shouldn't have please take it back amy replied theres no time for humility your plane is about to take off i said really you should keep it yours is already on the plane along with a few other things it took me a few moments to realize what she meant then i said one last final good bye to amy my ex sister.

CHAPTER 12

CLARIFICATION

12.1 QUOTATION MARKS

The proper use of quotation marks must be studied and learned, since some of their uses appear arbitrary and outside common sense.

The most common use of double quotation marks (" ") is to set off quoted words, phrases and sentences:

"If everbody minded their own business," said the Duchess in a hoarse growl, "the world would go round a great deal faster than it does."

"Then you would say what you mean," the March Hare went on.
" I do," Alice hastily replied: "at least--at least I mean what I say--that's the same thing, you know."

" Not the same thing a bit!" said the Hatter. "Why, you might just as well say that 'I see what I eat' is the same thing as 'I eat what I see'!"

Both quotes from Lewis Carroll's
Alice in Wonderland

In the last quote, single quotation marks are used to set off quoted material within a quote. Other examples of correct use of single quotation marks are:

"Shall I bring 'Rhyme of the Ancient Mariner' along with us?" she asked her brother.

Mrs. Green said, "The doctor told me, 'Go immediately to bed when you get home.'"

"If she said that to me," Katherine insisted, "I would

tell her, 'I never intend to speak to you again! Goodbye, Susan.'"

12.1.1 WRITING A DIALOGUE

When writing a dialogue, begin a new paragraph each time the speaker changes:

> "Do you know what time it is?" asked Jane. "I don't want to be late for my class."
> "Can't you see I'm busy?" snapped Mary. "Go into the kitchen if you want the time."
> "It's easy to see you're in a bad mood today," replied Jane.

Use quotation marks to enclose words used as words (sometimes italics are used for this purpose).

> "Judgment" had always been a difficult word for me to spell.

> Do you know what "abstruse" means?

> I always thought "nice" meant "particular" or "having exacting standards," but I know now it has acquired a much more general and vague meaning.

> "Horse and buggy" and "bread and butter" can be used as either adjectives or nouns.

If slang is used within more formal writing, the slang words or phrases should be set off with quotation marks.

> The "old boy" system is responsible for most promotions in today's corporate world.

> I thought she was a "knockout," which made it difficult to relate to her as the supervisor.

> Harrison's decision to leave the conference and to "stick his neck out" by flying to Jamaica was applauded by the rest of the participants.

When words are meant to have an unusual or special significance to the reader, for instance irony or humor, they are sometimes placed in quotation marks. This is, however, a practice to be avoided whenever possible. The reader should be able to get the intended meaning from the context.

*For years, women were not allowed to buy real estate
in order to "protect" them from unscrupulous dealers.*
(The writer is using somebody else's word; the use of
the quotation marks shows he or she does not believe
women needed protection.)

*The "conversation" resulted in one black eye and a bro-
ken arm.*

> *Our orders were always given as "suggestions."*

To set off titles of radio and TV shows, poems, stories, and
chapters in a book, use quotation marks. (Book, motion
picture, newspaper and magazine titles are underlined.)

> *The article "Moving South in the Summer Rain," by
> Jergen Smith in the <u>Southern News</u> attracted the attention
> of our editor.*

> *The assignment was "Childhood Development," chapter
> 18 of <u>Human Behavior</u>.*

> *My favorite essay by Montaigne is "On Silence."*

> *"I'm Gonna Wash that Man Right Out of My Hair" was
> the big hit song from <u>South Pacific</u>.*

> *Whitman's "Song of the Open Road" may be the most well-
> known poem from his <u>Leaves of Grass</u>.*

> *"Happy Days" led the TV ratings for years, didn't it?*

> *Jackson Miller's "What's Your Opinion?" on WNYB stirs
> plenty of controversy every Thursday night.*

> *"Jesu Joy of Man's Desiring" by J.S. Bach leaves you
> optimistic and glad to be alive.*

> *I saw it in the "Guide" in the Sunday <u>Times</u>.*

> *You will find Keats' "Ode to a Grecian Urn" in chapter
> 3, "The Romantic Era," in Lastly's <u>Selections from Great
> English Poets</u>.*

12.1.2 ERRORS TO AVOID

Be sure to remember that quotation marks always come in
pairs. Do not make the mistake of using only one set.

> *NO: "You'll never convince me to move to the city, said
> Thurman. I consider it an insane asylum."*

> YES: *"You'll never convince me to move to the city,"*
> *said Thurman. "I consider it an insane asylum."*
>
> NO: *"Idleness and pride tax with a heavier hand than*
> *kings and parliaments," Benjamin Franklin is sup-*
> *posed to have said. If we can get rid of the for-*
> *mer, we may easily bear the latter."*
>
> YES: *"Idleness and pride tax with a heavier hand than*
> *kings and parliaments," Benjamin Franklin is sup-*
> *posed to have said. "If we can get rid of the for-*
> *mer, we may easily bear the latter."*

When a quote consists of several sentences, do not put the quotation marks at the beginning and the end of each sentence; put them at the beginning and end of the entire quotation.

> NO: *"It was during his student days in Bonn that*
> *Beethoven fastened upon Schiller's poem." "The*
> *heady sense of liberation in the verses must have*
> *appealed to him." "They appealed to every Ger-*
> *man." --John Burke*
>
> YES: *"It was during his student days in Bonn that*
> *Beethoven fastened upon Schiller's poem. The*
> *heady sense of liberation in the verses must have*
> *appealed to him. They appealed to every Ger-*
> *man." --John Burke*

Instead of setting off a long quote with quotation marks, you may want to indent and single space it. If you do indent, do not use quotation marks:

> *We are not enemies, but friends. We must not be enemies.*
> *Though passion may have strained, it must not break,*
> *our bonds of affection. The mystic chords of memory,*
> *stretching from every battlefield and patriot grave to*
> *every living heart and hearthstone all over this broad*
> *land, will yet swell the chorus of the Union when again*
> *touched, as surely they will be, by the better angels*
> *of our nature. --Abraham Lincoln*
> *First Inaugural Address*

Be careful not to use quotation marks with indirect quotation:

> NO: *Mary wondered "if she would ever get over it."*
> YES: *Mary wondered if she would ever get over it.*

> NO: *The nurse asked "how long it had been since we had visited the doctor's office."*

> YES: *The nurse asked how long it had been since we had visited the doctor's office.*

> NO: *"My exercise teacher told me," Mary said, "'that I should do these back exercises fifteen minutes each day.'"*

> YES: *"My exercise teacher told me," Mary said, "that I should do these back exercises fifteen minutes each day."*

When you quote several paragraphs, it is not sufficient to place quotation marks at the beginning and ending of the entire quote. Place quotation marks at the <u>beginning of each paragraph</u>, but only <u>at the end of the last paragraph.</u> Here is an abbreviated quotation for an example:

> *"Here begins an odyssey through the world of classical mythology, starting with the creation of the world, proceeding to the divinities that once governed all aspects of human life....*

> *"It is true that themes similar to the classical may be found in almost any corpus of mythology...Even technology is not immune to the influence of Greece and Rome....*

> *"We need hardly mention the extent to which painters and sculptors... have used and adapted classical mythology to illustrate the past, to reveal the human body, to express romantic or antiromantic ideals, or to symbolize any particular point of view."*

Remember that commas and periods are always placed inside the quotation marks even if they are not actually part of the quote.

> NO: *"Life always gets colder near the summit", Nietzsche is purported to have said, "--the cold increases, responsibility grows".*

> YES: *"Life always gets colder near the summit," Nietzsche is purported to have said, "--the cold increases, responsibility grows."*

> NO: *"Get down here right away", John cried. "You'll miss the sunset if you don't".*

> YES: *"Get down here right away," John cried. "You'll miss the sunset if you don't."*

NO: *"If my dog could talk", Mary mused, "I'll bet he*
             would say, 'Take me for a walk right this minute'".

YES: *"If my dog could talk," Mary mused, "I'll bet he*
             would say, 'Take me for a walk right this minute.'"

Other marks of punctuation such as question marks, exclamation points, colons and semicolons go inside the quotation marks if they are part of the quoted material. If they are not part of the quote, however, they go outside the quotation mark. Be careful to distinguish between the guidelines for the comma and period, which always go inside the quotation marks, and those for the other marks of punctuation.

NO: *"I'll always love you"! she exclaimed happily.*

YES: *"I'll always love you!" she exclaimed happily.*

NO: *Did you hear her say, "He'll be there early?"*
           (The question mark belongs to the entire sentence and not to the quote alone.)

YES: *Did you hear her say, "He'll be there early"?*

NO: *She called down the stairs, "When are you coming"?*
           (The question mark belongs to the quote.)

YES: *She called down the stairs, "When are you coming?"*

NO: *"Ask not what your country can do for you"; said*
          Kennedy, "ask what you can do for your country:"
          a statement of genius, I think.
          (The semicolon is part of the quoted material; the colon is not part of the quote, but belongs to the entire sentence.)

YES: *"Ask not what your country can do for you;" said*
          Kennedy, "ask what you can do for your country":
          a statement of genius, I think.

NO: *"Let me out"! he cried.   "Don't you have any pity"?*

YES: *"Let me out!" he cried.   "Don't you have any pity?"*

Remember to use only one mark of punctuation at the end of a sentence ending with a quotation.

NO: *She thought out loud, "Will I ever finish this paper*
          in time for that class?".

YES: *She thought out loud, "Will I ever finish this paper*
          in time for that class?"

> *NO:* "Not the same thing a bit!", said the Hatter. "Why,
> you might just as well say that 'I see what I eat'
> is the same thing as 'I eat what I see'!".

> *YES:* "Not the same thing a bit!" said the Hatter. "Why,
> you might just as well say that "I see what I eat'
> is the same thing as 'I eat what I see'!"

12.2 THE APOSTROPHE

Use the apostophe to form contractions: to indicate that
letters or figures have been omitted:

can't (cannot)   *o'clock (of the clock)*

I'll (I will)   *it's (it is)*

memories of '42 (1942) *won't (will not)*

you've (you have)   *they're (they are)*

Notice that the apostrophe is <u>always</u> placed where a letter or
letters have been omitted. Avoid such careless errors as
writing wo'nt instead of won't, for example. Contractions are
generally not used in formal writing. They are found
primarily in speech and informal writing.

An apostrophe is also used to indicate the plural form of
letters, figures, and words that normally don't take a plural
form. In such cases it would be confusing to add only an
"s."

> *He quickly learned his <u>r's</u> and <u>s's</u>.*

> *Children have difficulties in remembering to dot their
> <u>i's</u> and cross their <u>t's</u>.*

> *Most of the <u>Ph.D.'s</u> and <u>M.D.'s</u> understand the new
> technology they are using for anticancer drugs.*

> *Her <u>2's</u> always looked like her <u>4's</u>.*

> *Marion used too many <u>the's</u> and <u>and's</u> in her last paper
> for English literature.*

Whenever possible, try to form plurals of numbers and of
single or multiple letters used as words, by adding only "s."

> *the ABCs*   *the 1940s*

12.2.1 PLACEMENT OF THE APOSTROPHE
TO INDICATE POSSESSION

In spoken English, the same pronunciation is used for the plural, singular, possessive, and plural possessive of most nouns. It is only by the context that the listener is able to tell the difference in the words used by the speaker. In written English, the spelling as well as the context tells the reader the meaning of the noun the writer is using. The writer has only to master the placement of the apostrophe so that the meaning is clearly conveyed to the reader. These words are pronounced alike but have different meanings:

PLURAL	SINGULAR POSSESSIVE	PLURAL POSSESSIVE
neighbors	*neighbor's*	*neighbors'*
doctors	*doctor's*	*doctors'*
weeks	*week's*	*weeks'*
sopranos	*soprano's*	*sopranos'*
civilizations	*civilization's*	*civilizations'*

If you aren't sure of the apostrophe's placement, you can determine it accurately by this simple test: change the possessive phrase into "belonging to" or an "of" phrase to discover the basic noun. You will find this a particularly useful trick for some of the more confusing possessive forms such as those on words that end in "s" or "es."

Keats' poem: The poem belonging to Keats.
Base noun is <u>*Keats*</u>; possessive is Keats' or Keats's, not Keat's or Keats'es.

The Joneses' house: The house of the Joneses (plural of Jones); Base is <u>*Joneses*</u>; possessive is Joneses', not Jones' or Jones'es.

Four months' pay: The pay of four months.
<u>*Months*</u> is base; possessive is months', not month's.

In two hours' time: In the time of two hours.
<u>*Hours*</u> is base; possessive is hours', not hour's.

The lioness' strength: The strength of the lioness.
Lioness is base; possessive is lioness' or lioness's, not
lioness'es or liones's.

It is anybody's guess: The guess of anybody.
Anybody is the base noun; possessive is anybody's not
anybodys' or anybodies'.

12.3 ITALICS

Italic is a particular kind of type used by printers. It is a
light, thin type that slants to the right. In writing or typing,
italic is indicated by underlining. Although its usage varies a
great deal, there are some general guidelines that should be
followed.

Italics are used most often to indicate the title of a play,
book, movie, long poem, newspaper, magazine, musical composition, work of art, ship, train or aircraft.

> *She had just read Kenneth Clark's Civilization.*
>
> *Leonardo da Vinci's most famous painting must certainly
> be La Gioconda, which we know as the Mona Lisa.*
> (Traditional titles or nicknames are not underlined.)

> *The New York Times (or New York Times) may be the
> best paper in the world.* (The name of the city assoc-
> iated with a newspaper and considered part of the title
> may or may not be italicized.)

> *Last night we saw La Traviata, an opera I'd go see again.*
>
> *My father would go to Europe each year on the Queen
> Elizabeth.*

> *Oliver was the most popular play on Broadway for many
> years.*
>
> *I read that Reader's Digest and TV Guide are the most
> successful magazines of all time.*

> *The Enola Gay dropped the first atomic bomb on Hiroshima.*
>
> *We are both looking forward to our trip to London on
> the Concorde.*

12.3.1 ERRORS TO AVOID

Reserve quotation marks for shorter parts of longer works such as stories, poems or chapters, and the titles of radio and TV shows. This helps distinguish the title of a book from a chapter, the name of an article from a magazine title and a poem from the collection in which it appears.

NO: *The Southern Predicament* that ran in the *Atlantic Monthly* in February received attention from us all.

YES: *"The Southern Predicament"* that ran in the *Atlantic Monthly* in February received attention from us all.

NO: *I advised them to read Song of Myself in Walt Whitman's Leaves of Grass.*

YES: *I advised them to read "Song of Myself" in Walt Whitman's Leaves of Grass.*

NO: *Chapter 6, The Marijuana Question, seems to me the most controversial part of Drugs Today by Himmel.*

YES: *Chapter 6, "The Marijuana Question," seems to me the most controversial part of Drugs Today by Himmel.*

Use italics to indicate a foreign word that has not yet become part of accepted English. Refer to your dictionary in order to be sure of the status of a particular word. Examples of familiar foreign words that are already part of our language and should not be italicized are:

a priori	*psyche*	*status quo*
cliché	*elan*	*ad hoc*
staccato	*trattoria*	*andante*
fait accompli	*ipso facto*	*rendezvous*
tete-a-tete	*dolce vita*	

Some foreign phrases and words that should be italicized are:

The Perellis all called "arividerci" as Daniel left.
(Italian for "farewell")

She'd always had a femme de chambre.
(French for "chambermaid")

Theirs was certainly a <u>marriage de convenance</u>.
(French for "marriage of convenience")

My motto in dealing with others is <u>nosce te ipsum.</u>
(Latin for "know thyself")

It is an attribute of our <u>Zeitgeist</u>.
(German for "spirit of the times")

When words are referred to as words, either quotation marks or italics can be used. (See "QUOTATION MARKS")

> *Mind your "p's" and "q's."*
>
> OR

Mind your <u>p's</u> and <u>q's</u>.

> *I'm never sure whether to use "infer" or "imply."*
>
> OR

I'm never sure whether to use <u>infer</u> or <u>imply</u>.

> *My "2's" and "4's" look similar.*
>
> OR

My <u>2's</u> and <u>4's</u> look similar.

Sometimes special emphasis is put on a word or phrase by underlining it or placing it in quotation marks. Minimize this practice whenever you can; try to indicate emphasis by word order or syntax, rather than by excessive underlining, which reflects laziness on the part of the writer.

> *She didn't ask John to come; she asked <u>me</u>.*
>
> *He did, after all, have a <u>religious</u> upbringing.*
>
> *It's <u>Time</u> that heals our wounds.*
>
> *You can't expect me to believe <u>that</u>.*

12.4 CAPITALIZATION

When a letter is capitalized, it calls special attention to itself. This attention should be for a good reason. There are standard uses for capital letters as well as much difference of opinion as to what should and should not be capitalized. In general, capitalize 1) all proper nouns, 2) the first word of a sentence, and 3) a direct quotation.

NAMES OF SHIPS, AIRCRAFT, SPACECRAFT AND TRAINS:

Apollo 13   *Mariner IV*
DC-10   *S.S. United States*
Sputnik II   *Boeing 707*

NAMES OF DEITIES:

God   *Jupiter*
Allah   *Holy Ghost*
Buddha   *Diana*
Jehovah   *Shiva*

GEOLOGICAL PERIODS:

Neolithic age   *Cenozoic era*
late Pleistocene times   *Age of Reptiles*
Ice Age   *Tertiary period*

NAMES OF ASTRONOMICAL BODIES:

Venus   *Big Dipper*
the Milky Way   *Halley's comet*
Ursa Major   *North Star*
Scorpio   *Deneb*
the Crab nebula   *Pleiades*

(Note that sun, moon and earth are not capitalized unless they are used with other astronomical terms that are capitalized.)

PERSONIFICATIONS:

Reliable *Nature* brought her promise of Spring.

Bring on *Melancholy* in his sad might.

Morning in the bowl of night has flung the stone/
that set the stars to flight.

HISTORICAL PERIODS:

the Middle Ages   World War I

Reign of Terror   Great Depression

Christian Era   Roaring Twenties

Age of Louis XIV   Renaissance

ORGANIZATION, ASSOCIATIONS AND INSTITUTIONS:

Girl Scouts of America   Ku Klux Klan

Young Men's Christian Association   North Atlantic Treaty Organization

New York Yankees   Kiwanis Club

Nazi Party   League of Women Voters

Smithsonian Institution   Unitarian Church

the Library of Congress   Common Market

the Illinois Central   New York Philharmonic

Franklin Glen High School

GOVERNMENT AND JUDICIAL GROUPS:

United States Court of Appeals   Committee on Foreign Affairs

New Jersey City Council   House of Commons

Senate   Parliament

Arkansas Supreme Court   House of Representatives

Peace Corps   Department of State

Municipal Court of Chicago   Iowa Board of Education

Census Bureau

A general term that accompanies a specific name is capitalized only if it follows the specific name. If it stands alone or comes before the word, it is put in lower case.

Washington State   the state of Washington

Senator Direksen   the senator from Illinois

Central Park   the park

Golden Gate Bridge	*the bridge*
President Andrew Jackson	*the president of the U.S.*
Pope John XXIII	*the pope*
Queen Elizabeth I	*the queen Elizabeth I*
Tropic of Capricorn	*thr tropics*
Glen Brook High School	*the high school in Glen Brook*
Monroe Doctrine	*the doctrine originated by Monroe*
the Milky Way Galaxy	*our galaxy the Milky Way*
the Mississippi River	*the river*
Easter Day	*the day we celebrated Easter*
Treaty of Versailles	*the treaty signed at Versailles*
Webster's Dictionary	*a dictionary by Webster*

Use a capital to start a sentence or a sentence fragment.

> *Our car would not start.*
>
> *When will you leave? I need to know right away.*
>
> *Never!*
>
> *Let me in! Right now!*

When a sentence appears within a sentence, start it with a capital.

> *The main question is, Where do we start?*
>
> *We had only one concern: When would we eat?*
>
> *My sister said, "I'll find the Monopoly set."*
>
> *He answered, "We can only stay a few minutes."*

In poetry, it is usual practice to capitalize the first word of each line even if the word comes in the middle of a sentence.

> *When I consider everything that grows*
> *Holds in perfection but a little moment,*
> *That this huge stage produceth naught but shows,*
> *Whereon the stars in secret influence comment.*
>
> > *--William Shakespeare*

She dwells with Beauty--Beauty that must die;
And Joy, whose hand is ever at his lips
Bidding Adieu.

--John Keats

The most important words of titles are capitalized. Those words not capitalized are conjunctions (e.g., _and_, _or_, _but_), articles (_a_, _the_, _and_), and short prepositions (e.g., _of_, _on_, _by_, _for_). The first and last word of a title must always be capitalized.

A Man for All Seasons	_Crime and Punishment_
Of Mice and Men	_Let Me In_
Rise of the West	_"What to Look For"_
Sonata in G-Minor	_"The Ever-Expanding West"_
Strange Life of Ivan Osokin	_Rubaiyat of Omar Khayyam_
"All in the Family"	_Symphony No. 41_
"Ode to Billy Joe"	_Piano Concerto No. 5_

12.5 HYPHENS

12.5.1 COMPOUND WORDS

There are literally hundreds of rules for the use of hyphens-- especially in compound words. The following are some of the most important, more dependable rules for hyphenation of compounds.

Hyphenate two or more words used as adjectives when you want to express the idea of a unit, _if_ they come before the word they modify. If, however, they follow the main word, they should not be hyphenated. (See "ADJECTIVES AND ADVERBS")

well-known man	_a man who is well known_
twelve-foot ceiling	_a ceiling of twelve feet_
up-to-date information	_he is up to date_
on-the-job training	_training is on the job_
thirst-quenching drink	_a drink that is thirst quenching_
cross-country skiing	_skiing cross country_
dewy-eyed child	_the child was dewy eyed_

well-meaning aunt	*his aunt was well meaning*
fine-tuned instrument	*the instrument was fine tuned*
above-mentioned form	*form mentioned above*
well-equipped car	*car seems well equipped*
interest-bearing ac-count	*an account that bears interest*
one-inch margin	*a margin of one inch*

There are exceptions. Some compound adjectives retain the hyphen even if they follow the word they modify. Some you should know are:

All words (nouns and adjectives) that start with "self":

self-reliant boy	*he is self-reliant*
self-supporting girl	*she is self-supporting*
self-cleaning oven	*it is self-cleaning*

All adjective compounds that start with "all":

all-encompassing book	*the book is all-encompassing*
all-purpose cleanser	*the cleanser is all-purpose*
all-inclusive fee	*the fee is all-inclusive*

All adjective compounds that start with "half";

half-done cake	*cake was half-done*
half-awake student	*student was half-awake*
half-explored territory	*territory is only half-ex-plored*

Compound adjectives that end in "ly" are not hyphenated before or after the word they modify.

highly developed muscles	*his muscles were highly dev-eloped*
interestingly formed rocks	*rocks that are interestingly formed*
evenly spread seeds	*the seeds are evenly spread*
lovingly guarded secrets	*my secrets are lovingly guarded*

In general, compound words that serve as nouns are not hyphenated.

Compare:

Problem solving (noun) *was his talent.*
He had a problem-solving (adjective) *talent.*

He was a master artist. (noun)
They worked at the master-artist (adjective) *shop.*

Mary is a foster child. (noun)
She lives at the foster-child (adjective) *home.*

12.5.2 EXCEPTIONS

All "in-laws" take a hyphen:

brother-in-law

mother-in-law

sisters-in-law

In addition, hyphens have other uses.

In a series of hyphenated words with a common ending, hyphens are carried over so it is not necessary to repeat the word each time:

Is it a 100- or 200-page book?

Do you want a two-, three- or five-column page?

They took six- and eight-cylinder cars along.

Both pro- and anti-American sentiment mounted.

Numbers from 21 to 99 are hyphenated when they are spelled out:

eighty-eight

sixty-three

two hundred forty-four

A hyphen is used to mean "up to and including" when used between numbers and dates:

1965-75   *10-15 people will be there*

He lived from 1919-1963

A hyphen is also used to avoid ambiguity when two capitalized names stand together:

> *the Boston-New York game*
>
> *the Chicago-London flight*
>
> *the Kramer-Lewis debate*
>
> *the Harrison-Jones marriage*

Many words still have prefixes that are set off by hyphens:

> *re-elect*   *ex-wife (always set "ex" off)*
>
> *pro-German*   *semi-independent*
>
> *anti-Nixon (prefixes added to proper nouns should always be hyphenated)*

12.6 BRACKETS

Brackets are probably the least used form of the pause. They do, however, serve some very useful purposes in clarifying material. When an editor needs to add corrections, explanations or comments, brackets are used:

> *"They [the Murphys] never meant to send that message to the White House."*   (Without the bracketed words, the reader would not know who had sent the message.)
>
> *Morris continued, "After the treaty was signed [The Treaty of Versailles], jubilation filled their hearts."*
>
> *The Times printed the senator's speech, which was addressed to "my countrymen, my countywomen [sic]."*   (The term [sic] indicates that the error is in the original source quoted; in this case "county-women" should have been "countrywomen.")

Brackets are also used to avoid confusion when it is necessary to use parentheses inside of parentheses.

> *Darkness fell so rapidly that she and her companion (June Morrison, who had herself traveled throughout Africa [particularly Nigeria])hardly noticed the transition from crystal blue to black.*
>
> *We know of a number of scholars who disagree with this theory (see Jackson Hewitt, To Earth's Center [Boston: Inkwell Press, 1953], pp. 614).*

12.7 NUMBERS

In writing, numbers can either be spelled out or be represented by the figures themselves. Although there is no definite rule, there are some guidelines that should be followed.

Most writers spell out numbers under 100 and use figures for 100 and over.

for eighteen years   *306 buildings*

eleven states   *only 514 more cars*

forty-five years old   *4,762 students*

ninety-nine percent   *I agree 100 percent*

two years ago   *100,486 football fans*

A number that starts a sentence should always be spelled out, even if it is over 100.

Three thousand forty-two voters selected Ross.

Nineteen seventy-five is a year I will never forget.

Eighty-five dollars did not seem like much to me for the fur hat.

Within the same paragraph, numbers that refer to the same category should be treated alike. Be consistent; be careful not to use *figures* for some and spell others out.

Forty-six men and 118 women joined the club last year. In comparison, the year before, thirty-five men and 56 women joined.

During the past eight years, we have owned more than 100 parakeets. Just two years ago, 12 of the birds received national notice for their ability to speak 3 or more languages. I heard of a bird in South America that speaks 125 languages.
(If the largest figure is over 100, use figures for all the numbers of that category to avoid having to write out long numbers.)

Very large numbers are usually spelled out if they are round numbers:

The earth may be 4 billion years old.

That house supposedly sold for $1 million. (Do not use "$" and "dollars" since they mean the same thing.)

Some baseball players make $2.5 million a year now.
            OR
Some make 2.5 million dollars now.

It is usually more clear to use figures when writing a fraction.

The brochure was printed on 9-by-12½-inch paper.

The board for the bed was .78 of an inch too short.

When Susan was in school, she had a 3.2 average.

Interest rates for borrowing money were at 17½ percent last week.

There are a number of different ways to write dates:

July 3, 1962   OR   *3 July 1962*

July third   OR   *the third of July*

nineteenth cen-   OR   *the 1800s*
  tury
the sixties   OR   *the '60s*

Write out ordinal numbers (fourth, twenty-third, etc.) rather than writing them as numbers with letter endings.

Whenever mentioning parts of a book, (page numbers, sections, chapters, exercises), use figures.

Please refer to page 184 in chapter 6 of your history book, if you want the answer to your question.

We found four case studies in section 8 of Jack's first-year law book.

The teacher assigned exercise 12 on page 235.

To form the plural of spelled-out numbers, follow the same rules you follow to form the plural of other nouns.

Will the number eighteens come forward, please?

He's in his thirties.

They came in twos and threes.

To form the plural of figures, add only " s. "

There could never be two 8½s.

The 1880s and the 1890s were exciting times in American history.

On the science quiz, there were three 100s, four 92s, six 85s, three 80s, and twelve 70s.

Addresses are usually written in figures:

189 Wellesley Drive, Cambridge, Massachusetts 01963

14 Mill Brook Road, Sumerset Glen, Iowa 23567

P.O. Box 583, Winding Ridge, Gloryville, W.Va.

2 East 125 Street OR 2 East 125th Street

When the numbers on the address can be spelled out in one or two words, it is also acceptable to spell them out.

One Park Avenue

Two Hundred West Lake Drive

Forty-One Fifth Avenue

Three Thousand Oaks Road

12.8 EXERCISES

QUOTATION MARKS

Correctly punctuate the following sentences.

1. Take an umbrella, said his mother, it looks like rain.
2. I haven't seen my old lady in five years, he exclaimed.
3. Can I write a comparative essay using To Autumn and Ode to a Nightingale for the assignment, asked the student.
4. My Favorite Things is a popular song from The Sound of Music, he remarked.
5. Do you understand the difference between overt and covert?
6. The washing machine went haywire this afternoon.
7. They wondered if they could do the job.
8. "Joseph locked the door"; said Andy "then, he put the key under the doormat".
9. You and Your Health is a popular show on WMCA.
10. Mary said "She is leaving for California tomorrow"!
11. "Don't ask any questions now", Susan exclaimed, "I'm trying to read".
12. "I can't believe it"! she exclaimed.
13. "Give me a match"! , she cried. "Don't you know it's dark in here?"
14. The article Iran After the Revolution appeared in last month's issue of The Middle East Journal.
15. "I can't begin to tell you what my day was like, said Karen. It all began when I missed the bus!"
16. "My history teacher suggested," Joe said, "'that I read Sinclair Lewis' Main Street.'"
17. Sitting in the dark she wondered "Will the lights ever come back on?"
18. February is always a spelling problem for me.
19. "It was after his trip to Europe that he decided to enroll in college." "It had been many years since he had been in school, but he truly wanted to return".
20. My aunt wanted to know "how many years it had been

12.8 EXERCISES

since we met last."

21. "Come over here, said Charles, I have something to show you."

22. "If he were here this moment", Linda said, "I know he would say, What's for dinner?"

23. I agree"; said Mark "its time to take a stand".

24. Please read Robert Frost's The Most of It in Chapter 15, Modern Poetry, in Gray's Anthology of Poetry.

25. Joan realized "it was time to leave the house".

THE APOSTROPHE

A. CONTRACTIONS --Write the contractions of the following:

1. she will,_____   4. does not, _____

2. shall not, _____   5. they have, _____

3. Class of 1981, _____   6. We are, _____

B. In the following sentences, make the necessary corrections. Also, note the reasons for your corrections.

1. This boat isnt yours. We sold our's last year to Roberts parents.

2. At 10 oclock theyll meet us at Macys department store.

3. Lindas sister was politically active in the 1960's.

4. In Ms. Greens first grade class, she had difficulty writing x's and learning her ABC's.

5. Wordsworths poem "the Solitary Reaper" was published in J. Mahoneys edition of The Romantic Poet"s.

6. Many of the defense attorneys witness' were afraid to appear at Johns trial.

7. "Its time to eat dinner" called James mother.

8. Arent you going to see if John's home so you can find out the results of Mondays game.

9. "Ode on a Grecian Urn," written by John Keats' is very famous. Ive read it at least twenty times.

10. Isn't it a shame that Peters team lost the game. They should have remembered their three Rs.

12.8 EXERCISES

C. <u>POSSESSION</u> --Write the possessive singular and the plural possessive of each of the following words:

1. lady,_____,_____
2. child, _____,_____
3. cashier, _____,_____
4. Filipino,_____,_____
5. country, _____,_____
6. James, _____,_____
7. knife, _____,_____
8. mouse,_____,_____
9. roof,_____,_____
10. attorney,_____,_____

ITALICS AND CAPITALIZATION

Correctly italicize and punctuate the following sentences.

1. I suggest you read Moral Symmetry in this weeks issue of The Nation.
2. People always refer to the sinking of the Titanic.
3. Although it was a cliché, he said "bon chance".
4. The Boston orchestra recently recorded Handel's Music for the Royal Fireworks.
5. The River by Memorial high school is polluted
6. The Washiongton Post recently published a controversial editorial Will the Suvivors Envy the Dead?
7. This year in English class you will be required to read John Milton's Paradise Lost
8. A photograph of the eclipse of the moon was printed in Photography
9. How many times has she seen Gone With the Wind at the Cinema II Theatre?
10. When reading his handwriting, it is difficult to distinguish his m's from his n's.
11. We were assigned Chapter 12, Abnormal Psychology, in

12.8 EXERCISES

our text, Introduction to Psychology.

12. Darkly clad in a robe, darkness descended over the William's mansion

13. After the Astronomy class we all knew how to locate the big dipper.

14. My brother said, "i'll repair the leak in the kitchen.

15. Throughout the Koran, allah is referred to.

16. The members of The House Un-American Activities Committee along with senator Joseph McCarthy did most of the investigating during the cold war.

17. The teacher asked, "Who read Great Expectations?"

18. It doesn't appear that the new york Yankees will be contenders in the world series this fall.

19. Trading in the common market is listed in the Wall Street Journal.

20. The state of the union address was given by president Ronald Reagan last week

HYPHENS

Make the necessary corrections in the following sentences. Briefly note the reasons for the hyphenation.

1. Gift giving was her nature.

2. She invited her mother in law to dinner Monday night.

3. He is a highly skilled artist.

4. The job was only half done.

5. The dictator was all powerful.

6. Many wanted to reelect the ex president.

7. The actor was well known.

8. Mary always lacked self confidence and willpower.

9. That is a little known fact.

10. The California New York game drew a large crowd.

11. Charles is a hard worker.

12. Does the professor want a two three or four page essay?

13. I was number twenty two on the line.

12.8 EXERCISES

14. The pro American sentiment weakened in mid September.

15. The well meaning citizen contacted the district attorney.

BRACKETS

Brackets are one form of the pause used in writing. Write five sentences where brackets are used. Substitute dashes, commas, and other forms of the pause, for these brackets. What effect does this have on the tone of the writing? Also try eliminating the brackets and the information enclosed in the brackets. What effect does this have on the writing?

NUMBERS

Write the following numbers as they would be expressed in formal writing.

1. We expected 329 members to attend the 3rd annual convention.

2. During the past 10 years, we have moved 22 times. We are now living at 225 Maple Street.

3. She won $2,000,000 as the 1st prize of the lottery.

4. Please reread page 183 of your text book; it summarizes all of Chapter 19.

5. The revolutions of the 1840's were a turning point in 19th Century European history.

6. They recently rented an apartment at 39 West 193rd Street.

7. They used to live at 1 5th Avenue.

8. 1,139 protestors attended the rally in Central Park even though the temperature reached 93°.

9. It was estimated that eighteen and one half percent of the population went abroad last year.

10. 1981 was a good year for the newspaper. Even though we printed our issues on nine-by-fourteen and one half inch paper, we sold a record amount of copies.

CHAPTER 13

SPELLING

At first glance, one would expect _blew_ and _sew_ to rhyme. Instead, _sew_ rhymes with _so_. If words were spelled the way they sound, one would expect _so_ to rhyme with _do_ instead of _dough_, and would never expect _do_ to rhyme with _blew_. Confusing isn't it?

Words are not always spelled phonetically, and it sometimes seems that spelling is totally illogical. However, in spelling there is usually only one correct form.

It is important to learn to spell properly. Poor spelling is usually a sign of haste or carelessness, and is often taken as a sign of ignorance or illiteracy. Yet learning to spell correctly is just more difficult for some people than for others. However it can be mastered with time and patience.

There are many helpful practices to improve spelling: using the dictionary, keeping a list of words that cause difficulty, familiarity with word origin, and studying the word list and the rules that follow.

If a writer has absolutely no idea how to spell a word, it obviously cannot be looked up. Yet in most spelling problems, the writer has a general idea of the spelling, but is not certain. Even if only the first few letters of the word are known, the author should be able to find it in the dictionary.

Example: To check the spelling of the word _"miscellaneous."_

The writer probably knows that _"misc-"_ are the first four letters of the word, and might even know a few more by sounding the word out. Although phonetics is not a reliable source for spelling, it can be helpful when using the dictionary. In this particular problem, it most likely is the ending _"-aneous"_ that gives the author difficulty. Since in the English language there are few words beginning with the letters *"misc-,"* the writer should have little trouble finding *"miscellaneous"* in the dictionary.

Example: To check the spelling of *"occasionally."*

Here, the writer is probably concerned with the number of c's and s's. If one looks up the word with the beginning *"oca-"* there is no listing. The logical choice is to check the word with two c's, which can be found a few spaces below. One can even skim the page when a general idea of the spelling is known.

When using the dictionary, be sure also that you have found the desired word, not a homonym or a word with a similar form, by checking the word's definition.

Simply enough, checking spelling is a matter of trial and error, so use the dictionary when you are not sure--and even sometimes when you feel you are certain.

13.1 WORD ANALYSIS

A basic knowledge of the English language, especially a familiarity with its numerous prefixes, can help build vocabulary and also strengthen spelling. For example, if one knows that "inter" means "between" and "intra" means "within," one is not likely to spell "intramural" "intermural." (The former means within the limits or limits of a city, college, etc.)

The following table lists some common Latin and Greek prefixes which are part of the foundation of the English language.

PREFIX	MEANING	ENGLISH WORD
ab-, a-, abs-	away, from	abstain
ad-	to, toward	adjacent
ante-	before	antecedent
anti-	against	antidote
bi-	two	bisect

PREFIX	MEANING	ENGLISH WORD
circum-	around	circumlocution
cata-, cat-, cath-	down	cataclysm
contra-	against	contrary
de-	down, from	decline
di-	twice	diatonic
dis-, di-	apart, away	dissolve
epi-, ep-, eph-	upon, among	epidemic
ex-, e-	out of, from	extricate
hyper-	beyond, over	hyperactive
hypo-	under, down, less	hypodermic
in-	in, into	instill
inter-	among, between	intercede
intra-	within	intramural
meta-, met-	beyond, along with	metaphysics
mono-	one	monolith
non-	no, not	nonsense
ob-	against	obstruct
para-, par-	beside	parallel
per-	through	permeate
pre-	before	prehistoric
pro-	before	project
super-	above	superior
tele-, tel-	across	television
trans-	far	transpose
ultra-	beyond	ultraviolet

13.2 SPELLING LISTS

There are some words that consistently give writers trouble. The list below contains 100 words that are commonly misspelled. In studying this list, each person will find that certain words are more troublesome than others. These in particular should be reviewed.

100 COMMONLY MISSPELLED WORDS

accommodate
achievement
acquire
among
apparent
argument
arguing
athletics
belief
believe
beneficial
benefited
bureau
business
category
comparative
conscious
controversial
definitely
definition
define
describe
description
despair
disastrous
effect
embarrass
environment
exaggerate
existence
existent
experience
explanation

February
height
immediately
interest
its, it's
led
lose
losing
marriage
mere
necessary
occasion
occurred
occurring
occurrence
opinion
opportunity
parallel
particular
performance
personnel, personal
possession
possible
practical
precede
prejudice
prepare
prevalent
principle
privilege
probably
proceed
procedure

profession
prominent
pursue
quiet
receive
receiving
recommend
referring
remember
repetition
rhythm
sense
separate
separation
similar
studying
succeed
succession
surprise
technique
then, than
their, they're, there
thorough
to, too, two
tomorrow
transferred
unnecessary
villain
write
writing

fascinate   *professor*

As a handy reference, it is a good idea to set aside an area in a notebook listing problem words. Add to it any new words that are persistent problems.

13.3 SPELLING RULES

13.3.1 PREFIXES

Prefixes (such as *dis-*, *mis-*, *in-*, *un-*, and *re-*) are added to words without doubling or dropping letters.

> *dis + appear = disappear*
>
> *dis + agree = disagree*
>
> *dis + service = disservice*
>
> *dis + solved = dissolved*
>
> *dis + appoint = disappoint*
>
> *dis + satisfied = dissatisfied*
>
> *mis + information = misinformation*
>
> *mis + spelled = misspelled*
>
> *mis + understand = misunderstand*
>
> *mis + led = misled*
>
> *in + capable = incapable*
>
> *in + definite = indefinite*
>
> *in + numerable = innumerable*
>
> *un + usual = unusual*
>
> *un + seen = unseen*
>
> *un + named = unnamed*
>
> *re + elect = re-elect*
>
> *re + search = research*

13.3.2 SUFFIXES

1. When forming adverbs from adjectives ending in *al*, the

ending becomes *ally*.

normal	*normally*
real	*really*
occasional	*occasionally*
legal	*legally*
royal	*royally*

2. Words ending in *n* keep the *n* when adding *ness*.

openness	*stubbornness*
suddenness	*brazenness*

3. All words ending in *ful* have only one *l*.

cupful	*cheerful*
forgetful	*doleful*
mouthful	*graceful*
helpful	*meaningful*
spoonful	*handful*

4. Add *ment* without changing the root word's spelling.

adjust + ment = adjustment

develop + ment = development

amaze + ment = amazement

5. Silent *"e"*.

When a suffix beginning with a vowel is added, a word ending in a silent *-e* generally drops the *-e*.

Example:

admire + able = admirable

allure + ing = alluring

believe + able = believable

come + ing = coming

dare + ing = daring

deplore + able = deplorable

desire + ous = desirous

explore + ation = exploration

fame + ous = famous

imagine + able = imaginable

move + able = movable

note + able = notable

However, the word retains the -*e* when a suffix beginning with a consonant is added.

Example:

arrange + ment = arrangement

glee + ful = gleeful

like + ness = likeness

spite + ful = spiteful

time + less = timeless

With *judgment*, *acknowledgment* and other words formed by adding *ment* to a word with a *dge* ending, the final *e* is usually dropped, although it is equally correct to retain it.

6. When adding *ous* or *able* to a word ending in *ge* or *ce*, keep the final *e* when adding the suffix. The *e* is retained to keep the soft sound of the *c* or *g*.

courageous	*manageable*
outrageous	*changeable*
advantageous	*traceable*

7. *IE + EI*

In words with *ie* or *ei*, where the sound is e, (long *ee*), use *i* before *e* except after *c*.

Examples: *i* before *e:*

believe	*reprieve*
chief	*shield*
niece	*siege*
pier	*wield*
priest	*yield*

Examples: Except after *c:*

ceiling	*deceive*
conceit	*perceive*
conceive	*receive*

The following words are some exceptions to the rule, and must be committed to memory.

either	*conscience*
leisure	*height*
neither	*forfeit*
seize	*neighbor*
weird	*reign*
freight	*weigh*

8. Except before <u>ing</u>, final <u>y</u> usually changes to <u>i</u>.

> *rely + ance = reliance*
> *study + ing = studying*
> *modify + er = modifier*
> *modify + ing = modifying*
> *amplify + ed = amplified*
> *amplify + er = amplifier*
> *amplify + ing = amplifying*

When preceded by a vowel, final <u>y</u> does not change to <u>i</u>.

> *annoying, annoyed*
> *destroying, destroyed, destroyer*
> *journeyman, journeyed, journeyer*

9. Doubling the Final Consonant:

In one syllable words which end in a single consonant and are preceded by a single vowel, double the final consonant before adding a suffix which begins with a vowel.

<u>Example</u>:

> *drop + ing = drop(p)ing*
> *clap + ed = clap(p)ed*
> *man + ish = man(n)ish*

$$snap + ed = snap(p)ed$$

$$quit + ing = quit(t)ing$$

But, when a suffix begins with a consonant, do not double the final consonant before adding the suffix.

Example:

$$man + hood = manhood$$

$$glad + ly = gladly$$

$$hap + ly = haply$$

$$fat + ness = fatness$$

$$.sin + ful = sinful$$

This is also the case in multisyllabic words which are accented on the final syllable and have endings as described above.

Example:

$$admit + ed = admitted$$

$$begin + ing = beginning$$

$$commit + ed = committed$$
$$BUT$$

$$commit + ment = commitment$$

However, in words with this type of ending, where the final syllable is not accented, the final consonant is not doubled.

Example:

$$happen + ing = happening$$

$$profit + able = profitable$$

$$comfort + ed = comforted$$

$$refer + ence = reference$$

$$confer + ence = conference$$

10. Only three words end in _ceed_ in English. They are _exceed, proceed,_ and _succeed._ All other "seed-sounding" words (except _supersede_) end in _cede_.

intercede	_recede_
concede	_accede_

secede   *precede*

13.4 PROOFREADING

The best way to improve spelling is to reread what has been written. In fact, many other writing problems can be avoided if the writer carefully rereads and revises. Remember, poor spelling is not something that must be lived with. With a little work, it can be greatly improved.

13.5 EXERCISES

A. Correctly complete the following words with the letters
    IE or *EI*.

    1. l _ _ sure   6. ap_ _ce
    2. p_ _rce   7. bel_ _ve
    3. s_ _ge   8. spec_ _s
    4. w_ _ld   9. conc_ _ve
    5. th_ _f   10. bes_ _ge

B. Change each word as indicated.

    1. love + able suffix = _____.
    2. engage + dis prefix = _____.
    3. legible + il prefix = _____.
    4. force + ful suffix = _____.
    5. stubborn + ness suffix = _____.
    6. sight + un prefix & ly suffix = _____.
    7. elect + re prefix = _____.
    8. brag + ing suffix = _____.
    9. prefer + ence suffix = _____.
    10. interpret + mis prefix = _____.
    11. plan + ing suffix = _____.
    12. benefit + ed suffix = _____.
    13. spoon + ful suffix = _____.
    14. final + ly suffix = _____.
    15. named + un prefix = _____.
    16. spite + ful suffix = _____.
    17. outrage + ous suffix = _____.
    18. mourn + ful suffix = _____.
    19. rectify + ed suffix = _____.
    20. clarify + ing suffix = _____.
    21. profit + able suffix = _____.
    22. equip + ment suffix = _____.
    23. concur + ing suffix = _____.

13.5 EXERCISES

24. marvel + <u>ous</u> suffix = _____ .

25. spell + <u>mis</u> prefix = _____ .

C. Change the following words to the plural form.

1. birch, _____
2. motto, _____
3. bay, _____
4. self, _____
5. sheriff, _____
6. lady, _____
7. focus, _____
8. alto, _____
9. carry, _____
10. fly, _____
11. relay, _____
12. employ, _____
13. oasis, _____
14. ox, _____
15. studio, _____

D. Proofread the following sentences and make the necessary corrections.

1. She exaggerates there arguments all of the time.
2. She couldn't except the gift, its to expensive.
3. I can't believe they decieved her.
4. <u>A Seperate Peace</u>, by John Knowles, is a fascenating novel.
5. The sucession of the southern states caused the Civil War.
6. If you want a job you must aply in the personal departement.
7. Its important that you arrive immediately.
8. Thats an ambigous statement.

13.5 EXERCISES

9. Everyones day of judgement comes.

10. Tomorrow I will give you a suprise.

11. I always complement her on her fine cloths.

12. The proffessor is retiring in Febuary.

13. He persued his goal by studying hard.

14. I wanted to see that preformance more then the others.

15. The villan stole all their posessions.

16. She proceded to the alter.

17. It was a rare opprotunity to meet the incumbent senator from Vermont.

18. The cite of the capital building was quite beautiful .

19. The morale of the story was quiet clear.

20. Weather or not you attend is your dicision.

INDEX

99
recognizing, 91-93
superlative, 93, 95-97
use of infinitive as, 126, 127
with two acceptable forms,
92, 93
without *ly* ending, 91
Advice, advise, 9
Affect, effect, 10
After, as subordinating conjunction, 114
Agreement:
defined, 80
exercises, 86, 87
intervening words, 80, 81
of appositive, 51
of pronoun and antecedent,
51, 64
relative pronouns as subject,
52
singular subjects joined by
and or *or,* 82, 119
singular subjects joined
titles of single works as subjects, 83
with expletives, 124
with verb, 80-83
All:
as indefinite pronoun, 55
hyphen with, 210
All ready, already, 10
Allusion, illusion, 10
Almost:
adverb, 91
misplacement of, 133
Already, all ready, 10
Altar, alter, 10
Although:
as connector, 161
as subordinating conjunction,
114
Ambiguous reference of pronouns:
defined, 134
exercises, 149
An, a, 99, 100
Analogy:
defined, 165
exercise, 170
in developing paragraphs, 165
And:

as connector, 161
as coordinating conjunction,
110
beginning a sentence with,
111
capitalization of, 209
compound subjects, 119
connective pair, with *but,* 112
correlative conjunction, 112
parallel structure with, 137
punctuation with, 180, 183,
184
Anecdote:
defined, 164
exercise, 169
in developing paragraphs,
164
Anglicization of foreign words,
36, 204
Another, as indefinite pronoun,
55
Antecedent:
agreement with pronoun, 64
ambiguous reference to, 134
defined, 64
Antonyms, defined, 19,20,22
Anybody, anyone, as indefinite
pronouns, 55
Apostrophe, 201-203
contractions, 210
exercises, 217, 218
in plural forms, 201
to form possessives, 36, 37,
202, 203
with compounds, 43
with nouns in joint possession, 40, 41
with plurals ending in *s* or
z sound, 202, 203
with singulars ending in *s*
or *z* sound, 37
with words not ending in *s*
or *z* sound, 36, 37
Appear:
as copulative verb, 122
with adjectives, 98, 123
Appositive:
after a possessive, 42, 43
agreement, 51, 52
and colon, 177

plural forms, 28
Colon, 177-179
    after salutation in business letter, 178
    and capitalization, 177, 178
    and non-restrictive elements, 177
    and sentence fragments, 140
    before a list, 179
    before a quotation, 178
    between main clauses, 177
    defined, 177
    distinguished from semicolon, 177
    exercise, 192, 194
    inciting references, 179
    placement of, with quotation marks, 200
    replaced by comma, 177
    replaced by period, 177
    to correct run-on sentence, 141
    to introduce a series, 178
Comma, 182-190
    after abbreviations, 186
    after interjections, 175, 186
    after verbals, 184
    and run-on sentences, 140
    and sentence fragments, 140
    before coordinating conjunctions joining main clauses, 111, 185
    between items in series, 183, 184
    comma splice, 141
    definition, 182
    in addresses, 187
    in direct address, 187
    position with parentheses, 180
    position with question marks, 174
    position with quotation marks, 199
    reading aloud to find proper placement of, 171, 172
    superfluous, 183-186, 188, 189
    tag questions, 187
    to replace colon, 177
    to separate clauses, 129, 183
    to separate compound sentences, 185, 186
    to set off contrasting elements, 189
    to set off direct quotations, 189
    to set off geographical names, and on dates, addresses and letters, 179, 187, 190
    to set off interrupting material, 186-188
    to set off non-restrictive elements, 188
    to set off parenthetical elements, 187
    to set off transitional elements, 187
    used to prevent misreading, 184, 185
    use of dash in place of, 176
    use with reflexive pronouns, 57
    with a long introductory phrase, 184, 185
    with other punctuation, 174, 180, 199
Comma splice, defined, 141
Command:
    and sentence order, 124
    in imperative mood, 154
    in subjunctive mood, 154
    structure, 119
Comparative:
    defined, 93
    listed in dictionary, 19
    use of, 93-98
    (*see also* comparison)
Comparison:
    defined, 93
    degrees of, 93, 96
    endings, 93
    errors to avoid, 97
    exercises, 102, 103
    forms for, adjectives and adverbs, 93-95
    irregular forms, 94, 95
    with *"other"*, *"else"* or *"of all"*, 97, 98

201
Contrasted elements, comma
used with, 189
Contrast, in paragraph development, 164
Coordinating conjunctions, 110,
111
at beginning of sentences,
111
connecting items in a series,
183, 184
connecting main clauses, 111
defined, 110
errors to avoid, 111
exercise, 116
parallel structure with, 111
used in pairs(*correlatives*),
112
Coordination:
defined, 110
distinguished from subordination, 114
Copulative verb:
and adjective, 123
complement of, 122, 123
defined, 122
exercises, 146, 147
nominal as complement, 123
sentence order, 123, 124
subject of, 122
Correct meaning, 14
Correlative conjunctions, 112,
113
defined, 112
errors to avoid, 113
exercise, 116
parallel structure, 112
Council, consul, counsel, 11
Countable nouns, 28, 29
Counsel, consul, council, 11
Course, coarse, 11

Dangling modifier:
correction of, 130-133

defined, 128
Dangling participle:
defined, 130
exercise, 149
Dash:
before the author of a quotation, 177
defined, 176
exercise, 193, 194
formation on typewriter, 176
to indicate a sudden break,
176
to replace parenthesis, 176
to summarize, in a series,
176
Dates, writing of, 190, 214
Days, months, capitalization of,
26
Decent, descent, 11
Definite article, 99, 100
Definition, in developing paragraphs, 164
Definitions, in dictionaries, 19,
20
Degrees of comparison, 93, 96
Deity, capitalization of, 206
Deletions, in manuscript, 2
Demonstrative pronouns, 54, 55
as adjectives, 54, 55
exercise, 66
possession with, 62
Denotation and conotation, 15,
16
Descent, decent, 11
Detail, irrelevant, in paragraph
development, 165, 166
Development of paper, 5-8
Development of paragraphs, 158,
164, 165, 169
Device, devise, 11
Diacritical marks:
defined, 18
example, 19
Dialogue:
informal words in, 196
indentation of, 196
quotation marks, 195-201
paragraphing of, 196
sentence fragments in, 138
Diction:

tory phrase, 184
dash, 176
overuse of italics for, 205
quotation marks used for, 196, 205
reflexive pronouns, 56, 57
through repetition, 144
topic sentence, 160
summarizing sentence in paragraphs, 159
underlining, 205
use of voice for, 155, 156
wordiness used, 144
Es and *s*, in forming plurals, 34, 35
Etymology:
defined, 20
exercise, 23
in the dictionary, 20
Even, misplacement of, 133
Everybody, everyone, as indefinite pronoun, 55
Examples:
exercise, 169
in developing paragraphs, 164
Except, accept, 9
Exclamation point:
after interjections, 175
and quotation marks, 200
defined, 174
exercises, 191, 194
instead of question mark, 175
overuse of, 175
use within dash, 176
with parentheses, 180
Exclamations, and sentence fragments, 140
Expletives, defined, 63, 124

Facts:
exercise, 169

in developing paragraphs, 164
Fair, fare, 11
Farther, further, 95
Faulty coordination:
connection with conjunctions, 114
exercise, 117
Fem., 19
Few, as indefinite pronoun, 55
Figurative language:
definition, 153
exercise, 157
figures of speech, 153
mood, 154, 155
voice, 155, 156
Figures of speech:
defined, 153
exercise, 157
types, 153
Final consonant, doubling before suffix, 228, 229
Final *e*, dropping before adding suffix, 226
Final *y*:
before plural endings, 34
in spelling, 228
For:
and semicolon, 180, 181
and sentence order, 128
as coordinating conjunction, 110, 111
preposition, 104
Foreign words:
Anglicized, no italics, 36, 204
italicized, 204
phrases, 20
plural forms, 36
For example, as transitional phrase, 112
Form changes (inflection):
of adjectives and adverbs, 93-96
of nouns, 33-37
of pronouns, 50-52
of verbs, 70, 71
Forth, fourth, 12
Fractions, writing, 214
Fragments, sentence, 138-140

Ideas:
repetition in a paragraph,
163
similarity, parallel structure
of, 136-138
smooth flow, lack of, 142,
143
(*see also* Clarity)
Idiomatic expressions, using
"of" phrase, 38-41
Idiomatic language, 20, 21
Idiomatic prepositions:
defined, 106, 107
exercise, 109
list of, 107, 108
Ie, ei, in spelling, 227, 228
If, as subordinating conjunction,
114
If clause, and subjunctive mood,
154
If...then:
connective pair, 137
correlative conjunctions, 113
Illusion, allusion, 10
Immigrate, emigrate, 11
Imminent, immanent, eminent,
11
Imperative mood:
defined, 154
exercise, 157
Improper formation of reflexive
pronouns, 57
In addition:
and semicolon, 181
as connector, 161
as transitional phrase, 112
In addition to, as group preposition, 105
Inanimate possession, 37-41
Indeed, as a conjunctive adverb,
112
Indefinite article, 99, 100
Indefinite pronouns:
agreement, 56
defined, 55, 56
Indentation:
in dialogue, 196
of long quotations, 198
of paragraphs, 2
Indicative mood:

defined, 154
exercise, 157
Indirect object:
and pronouns, 60, 121
and sentence order, 124
defined, 121
exercise, 146, 147
Indirect quotes:
and commas, 189
and quotation marks, 198
Infinitive:
as adjective, 84
as adverb, 84
as noun, 84
as subject, 118
defined, 84
exercise, 88
in phrases, 127
tenses of, 85
Infinitive phrase:
as adjective or adverb, 127
as noun, 127
defined, 127
exercise, 147, 148
Infinitive verb, and pronoun,
60
Inflection:
defined, 33
indicated in dictionary, 19
of adjectives and adverbs,
93-96
of nouns, 33, 34
of pronouns, 50-52
of verbs, 70, 71
Intr., 19
Interj., 19
Interjections:
and exclamation point, 175
defined, 175
followed by comma, 175
Interrogative pronouns:
defined, 53, 54
exercise, 66
Intransitive verb:
and adverbs, 122
and complements, 121
defined, 121
exercise, 146, 147
subject of, 122
Introduction of the paper, 7

as ending of adverbs and adjectives, 91-93
in hyphenation, 210

Main clauses:
joined by coordinating con-junction, 110, 111
separated by colon, 177
separated by semicolon, 180, 181
Manuscript form, 2, 3
Many, as indefinite pronoun, 55
Masc., 19
Mass nouns, 28, 29
Mechanics of writing, 3
Merely, misplacement of, 133
Metaphor:
defined, 153
exercise, 157
mixed metaphor, 153
Misplaced modifiers, 131-133
defined, 131
exercise, 149
Mixed metaphor, defined, 153
Modifier:
and commas, 188
and complete subject, 119
and gerunds, 127
defined, 90, 91
in infinitive phrase, 127
in participial phrase, 127
in prepositional phrase, 126
misplaced, 131-133
non-restrictive, 188
of pronouns, 127
restrictive, 188
Modify, defined, 90, 91
Mood:
defined, 154, 155
exercise, 157
imperative, 154
indicative, 154
subjunctive, 154, 155

Moral, morale, 12
More, as indefinite pronoun, 55
comparative form, 95, 96
Moreover:
and semicolon, 181
as a conjunctive adverb, 112
as connector, 161
as coordinating conjunction, 110, 111
Most, as indefinite pronoun, 55
superlative with, 95, 96

N., 18
Nearly:
adverb, 93
misplacement of, 133
Neither:
as correlative conjunction, 113
part of connective pair, with *nor*, 137
Neither...nor:
and semicolon, 180, 181
as connectives, 137
as correlative conjunctions, 113
joining two subjects, 82
Never the less, as a conjunctive adverb, 112
Nobody, no one, as indefinite pronouns, 55
Nominal:
as complement of copulative verb, 123
defined, 118
Nominative case, (*see* subjective case):
of nouns, 33
Noncountable nouns, 28, 29
plural forms of, 29
Non-restrictive elements:
and commas, 188
defined, 188

suffixes, 225-229
suffixes beginning with consonants, 227
suffixes beginning with vowels, 226
word analysis, 222
y before *ing*, 228
Splice, comma, defined, 141
Standard paper size, 2
Stationary, stationery, 13
Still:
    and semicolon, 181
    as conjunctive adverb, 91, 112
Stops:
    defined, 172
    exclamation point, 174, 175
    period, 172, 173
    question mark, 173, 174
Straight, strait, 13
Style:
    active voice, 155, 156
    choppy sentences, 142, 143
    effective use of semicolon, 181
    exercise, 149-152, 157
    figurative language, 153-156
    rambling sentences, 145
    smooth transition between paragraphs, 161-164
    use of colon for dramatic tension, 177
    use of quotation marks to emphasize words, 196
    use of repetition, 144, 168
    use of sentence fragments, 140
    use of semicolons, 180
    wordiness, 144
    voice, 155, 156
Subject:
    agreement with verb, 80-83
    and copulative verb, 122
    and intransitive verb, 122
    and predicate, 118-120
    case, 58, 59
    complete, 119
    compound, 119
    defined, 118
    exercise, 146, 147, 157
    in compound sentences, 185

infinitive as, 118
joining two, 82
nominals, 118
of clause, pronoun as, 52, 53, 129
phrase as, 118
position in sentence, 123, 124
pronoun as, 118
pronoun case, 51, 58, 59
pronoun with verb, 51
relative pronoun as, 52
sentence fragment, 138
sentence order, 123-125
shifts in, 155, 156
simple, 118
use of quotations as, 189
use of reflexive pronouns for emphasis, after, 56
voice, 155
Subjective case:
    after "*to be*", 58, 59
    of pronouns, 50, 58-60
Subjunctive mood:
    defined, 154
    exercise, 157
    in "*if*" clauses, 154
    in "*that*" clauses, 154
    main clauses, 154, 155
    "*to be*" used in, 155
Subordinate clauses, introduced by subordinate conjunctions, 114
Subordinate conjunctions:
    defined, 114
    exercise, 116
Subordination, 114, 115
Such, as pointer, 54
Suffixes:
    spelling rules, 225-229
    used to convert adverbs to adjectives, 225, 226
Summarizing sentence:
    defined, 159
Superfluous commas, 182
    after adjective in combinations, 183
    after a short introductory phrase, 184
    before final item in a series, 183, 184